FLC
RIS

Medical Conditions

Medical Conditions

A Guide for the Early Years

Pam Dewis

continuum

Continuum International Publishing Group

The Tower Building
11 York Road
SE1 7NX

80 Maiden Lane, Suite 704
New York, NY 10038

www.continuumbooks.com

© Pam Dewis 2007

British Library Cataloguing-in-Publication Data
A catalogue record for this book is available from the British
Library.

ISBN: 0826484751 (paperback)

Library of Congress Cataloging-in-Publication Data
A catalog record for this book is available from the Library of
Congress.

Typeset by Fakenham Photosetting, Norfolk
Printed and bound in Great Britain by Ashford Colour Press,
Gosport, Hampshire

Contents

Medical Conditions

Contents

Introduction

There have been increasing levels of recognition and support for children with special educational needs (SEN) in recent years. A range of legislation and the introduction of the SEN Code of Practice (DfE 1994, DfES 2001a) have underpinned the development of specific support for children with learning difficulties across the range of educational provision. This development has been based on a set of principles that emphasize partnership with parents and children, and between schools, the local authority (LA) and other agencies, as key factors in supporting effective service delivery to children with SEN and their families.

Within the Code of Practice different areas of learning difficulties have been identified. The areas are, however, interlinked and it is acknowledged that there exists 'a wide spectrum of special educational needs that are frequently interrelated' (DfES 2001a: 7:52). Currently, four areas of SEN and requirements are identified:

- ◆ Communication and interaction
- ◆ Cognition and learning
- ◆ Behaviour, emotional and social development
- ◆ Sensory and/or physical

(DfES 2001a: 7:52)

Medical Conditions

Medical conditions are also discussed. It is made clear, however, that a medical condition does not in itself mean that a child has SEN. Instead, it is the impact of the condition (either directly because of the condition or indirectly because of the psychological impact of illness, treatment or other aspects of the condition) on the child's learning ability, and social and emotional development that may lead to SEN.

This book is mainly concerned with children who have needs arising from a medical condition, affecting either their physical and/or their mental health, and who require additional support and care in early years settings. The impact of having a medical condition on learning and development will be discussed, along with the different levels of intervention and support for children with medical conditions with associated SEN, and their families. The role of the Code of Practice (DfES 2001a) and other relevant legislation and policy in supporting children, families, settings and practitioners will be outlined. Discussion will then ensue on the role of early years practitioners and settings in supporting children with medical conditions and their families. This will be discussed in the context of partnership working, including partnerships with children and parents, and multi-agency and multi-disciplinary professionals, aimed at supporting children's holistic development within the framework of current practice.

This book is aimed at early years practitioners, their managers, students and tutors on early years courses and parents interested in developing their understanding of SEN. In the context of this book, 'early years' will refer to children aged 0–8 years old, in children's centres, nurseries, pre-schools, schools, at home or that of a childminder, and any other setting where children spend time. 'Early years practitioner' refers to anyone working in these types of settings in any capacity and could include teachers, teaching assistants, nursery nurses, playworkers, pre-school workers and volunteers.

In this book you will find case examples to illustrate some of the issues raised; points for reflection or discussion; self-assessment exercises; and action points to encourage you to gather information or resources to help you develop your skills in supporting children with medical conditions. These aspects of the book are intended to help you extend your understanding and to reflect on your own stage of development in this area.

Throughout the book the terms 'she' and 'he' and so on are used randomly to avoid the more clumsy s/he and him/her. Where 'parents' are referred to, this covers all those who assume parenting responsibilities including natural, adoptive and foster parents, guardians and carers.

1

Access to Early Years Education and Care for Children with Medical Conditions

In the event of effective and efficient support, children with medical conditions can enjoy optimal health, play and learning alongside their peers, and gain maximum access to both curricular and extra-curricular activities. Some children will need very little support, whereas others will require highly specialist care necessitating the employment of health personnel.

In this chapter, examples will be given of needs arising from medical conditions, which, in the absence of supportive responses, could limit children's access to and inclusion in early years settings, as defined in the Introduction. The chapter will highlight how such needs are often associated with SEN and/or disability and how some medical conditions generate more complex needs than others. Pertinent issues relevant to inclusive education and care for children with medical conditions will also be discussed.

Learning outcomes

When you have read this chapter, you should be able to:

♦ Give examples of needs arising from medical conditions

♦ Describe the overlap between medical conditions, disability and SEN

♦ Briefly explain why some children with medical conditions may be denied access to early years education and care settings despite the Disability Discrimination Act 1995

♦ Give examples of formal education provision for children with medical conditions

♦ Understand some pertinent issues relevant to inclusive education and care

Needs arising from medical conditions

Children with medical conditions may have one or, possibly, a combination of two or more of the following needs:

♦ Dietary modification – a child with diabetes or other metabolic disorders

♦ Help with feeding – a child who has problems eating and drinking or has a nasogastric tube or gastrostomy

♦ Wheelchair access

- Assistance with toileting
- Assistance with bladder emptying through catheterization
- Administration of medicines
- Maintenance of a clear airway – a child requiring regular suctioning of a tracheostomy, for example
- Infection control – a child with leukaemia and/or receiving steroid treatment
- Regular monitoring
- First aid

(This list is used for illustrative purposes only and is by no means exhaustive.)

As well as generating medical needs and needs associated with mobility, as per the above list, medical conditions can also give rise to problems around behaviour, emotional and social development (see Chapter 2).

Short-term illness or injury

It is important, at this juncture, to point out that a child need not necessarily have a medical condition to have such needs as those listed above. Short-term illness or injury can also generate such needs; for example, the need for medicine to be administered in early years settings or the need for help with mobility, albeit on a temporary basis. This book, however, is concerned with children whose needs arise from long-term, although not necessarily permanent, medical conditions.

Medical conditions with associated SEN and/ or disability

Some children with medical conditions will have associated SEN and/or disability. The model below, adapted from Carlin (2005), illustrates this point:

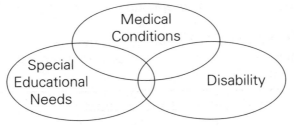

Fig 1.1
(adapted from Carlin 2005: 8)

It must be emphasized at this point, that such overlap occurs in some but certainly not all cases. A substantial number of children with a medical condition will not have SEN or disability. Conversely, many will have one or both. As such, where discussion within this book pertains to SEN and/or disability, this will naturally include some children with a medical condition. As already mentioned in the Introduction, the SEN Code of Practice stipulates that a child with a medical condition will only be considered to have SEN in the event of that condition affecting her ability to learn, either directly or indirectly (DfES 2001a). Direct and indirect effects of medical conditions on children's learning capacity will be explored in the next chapter.

Medical Conditions

While, in practice, it is sometimes assumed that if a child has a medical condition she must also have SEN, especially with regard to conditions such as epilepsy, others are not considered to have SEN, when in actual fact they do. In the main, those children whose medical condition obviously affects their physical and/or cognitive functioning are most likely to be deemed to have SEN (Closs 2000). As a consequence, children with less obvious medical conditions may miss out on support that could enhance their education (Closs 2000).

The following case example illustrates how even conditions of the brain do not necessarily mean that a child has SEN.

Case example: Kiranjit, 6 years

Kiranjit was diagnosed with idiopathic epilepsy at the age of 2 years. She is the only one in her family who has the condition. She attends the local primary school where there are three other children with epilepsy. Kiranjit's epilepsy is very well controlled with anti-epileptic medication which she takes twice a day: morning, before going to school, and evening. She is seen regularly by a paediatric neurologist and epilepsy specialist nurse. Kiranjit has convulsive seizures, however, given that the condition is well controlled, these are very few and far between nowadays. During her first week at school, Kiranjit had two seizures. Teachers and other staff at the school are trained in the first-aid treatment of epilepsy and also know when to summon medical assistance, so they

---

were able to look after her. They were concerned, however, that the condition might get in the way of her education, given its apparent severity. Kiranjit's mother informed the staff that Kiranjit had been seizure-free for four months prior to this episode and had been feeling very tired since starting full-time education. She explained that tiredness has been known to trigger Kiranjit's seizures. Kiranjit hasn't had any seizures during school hours since this episode. She is not considered to have SEN, despite having epilepsy. She loves school, is very popular with her peers and is making excellent educational progress.

Medical conditions with associated disability

Some medical conditions, for example brittle asthma or cystic fibrosis, may render a child disabled under the terms of the Disability Discrimination Act 1995, hereafter referred to as the DDA. The DDA defines a person as having a disability if he has 'a physical or mental impairment which has a substantial and long-term adverse effect on his ability to carry out normal day to day activities' (DDA 1995, Part 1 (1)).

It is difficult to apply the DDA definition of disability to very young children in that it is not always possible to determine whether a child's difficulties will be long-term. However, the need for early intervention and support remains crucial which is why the government has produced the following working definition of disability for children from birth to their third birthday:

Medical Conditions

> A child under three years shall be considered disabled if he/she:
>
> (i) s experiencing significant developmental impairment or delays, in one or more of the areas of cognitive development, sensory or physical development, communication development, social, behavioural or emotional development; or
>
> (ii) has a condition which has a high probability of resulting in delay.
>
> (DfES 2003a: 7)

The incidence of disability among the older child population is estimated at between three and five per cent (DfES 2003a). It is difficult, however, to predict the number of children, in any one area, likely to fit the government's working definition for very young children. Despite this, it is proposed, subject to local factors, that planners can expect to be able to identify around three per cent in any one locality (DfES 2003a).

It is important to note that a great many children with disabilities can attend, and benefit from attending, early years settings, with little need for resources beyond those they use to facilitate daily living, such as a wheelchair, for instance.

Needs continuum

Needs arising from medical conditions range from relatively basic to complex, depending on the nature and severity of the condition. Most children with medical conditions take regular medication which enables them to lead a normal life. Sometimes, however, children's needs are less straightforward.

Children with diabetes, for example, have several needs, including dietary modification, medication and first aid. Then there are children whose needs, due to the seriousness of their condition, are very complicated, in that they experience myriad difficulties, including absence and fatigue and/or the need for sophisticated medical intervention such as technology to sustain life. Sadly, at the extreme end of this continuum, there are children who are terminally ill and receiving palliative care. Many such children attend early years settings and require a great deal of support in order to do so.

The following case examples illustrate different degrees of need:

Case examples: Sally, 7 years and Gemma, 2 years, 6 months

Sally suffers from Type 1 diabetes. She requires an insulin injection twice a day. However, these do not need to be given during school hours. She also needs to eat regularly, including eating snacks during class time and prior to physical activity. She must also check her blood glucose level during the school lunch break and before PE. Sally invariably needs prompting to eat her snack because she has a tendency to become very engrossed in activities and therefore forgets. It is very important that she is reminded to eat lest she experience a hypoglycaemic episode. Sally can perform her own blood glucose test but finds it unpleasant and will therefore avoid doing

---

it if at all possible. A member of staff is responsible for reminding Sally to eat her snacks and for supervising her in testing her blood glucose level, not only to make sure that she does so, but also, to support her emotionally, given how unpleasant she finds the procedure.

Gemma has cerebral palsy. Her symptoms are severe in that she needs help in day-to-day tasks. She also shows delay in her cognitive development. Gemma is unable to walk unaided and requires regular physiotherapy and speech therapy. Although Gemma's needs are complex, her parents are very keen for her to attend the local pre-school so that she can interact with other children as well as enjoy all the other well known benefits of early education. Given the complexity of Gemma's needs, a request has already been made, by the health service, in agreement with her parents, for a statutory assessment of SEN by the LA with a view to a statement being drawn up.

Admission to early years settings

Children with medical conditions have the same rights of admission to early years settings as other children, as long as their condition does not pose a risk to the health and safety of staff and other children (DfES 2005). Having said this, however, settings continue to refuse admission to children on the grounds of being unable to cater for their needs. Children with allergic conditions, for example, are often refused admission, to pre-school settings especially, as are children who need frequent toileting or nappy changes.

Case example: Carla, 3 years

Carla is allergic to nuts. Because of this she occasionally needs emergency treatment by injection and must avoid foods containing nuts of any sort. These are the only needs arising from her condition. She does not have SEN or disability. The local pre-school has refused to admit Carla on the perceived grounds that staff should not be expected to be involved in administering injections to children. Carla's parents are distraught. They had not anticipated this response and don't know what to say to Carla who is very excited at the prospect of starting play school with her friends.

School-age children with SEN or disability have their rights of admission protected under Part 4 of the Education Act 1996, as amended by the Special Educational Needs and Disability Act (SENDA) 2001, and Part 4 of the DDA 1995, as amended by SENDA 2001, respectively. Pre-school age children with a disability have their rights of admission protected under Part 3 of the DDA (these Acts will be given further consideration in Chapter 3).

A substantial number of children gaining protection under these Acts are those with medical conditions. However, the rights of admission to early years settings for children like Carla above, who have a medical condition without associated SEN and/or disability, are not protected by legislative duties. A child whose life is significantly affected by asthma and/or eczema, for example, even where she is eligible for Disability Living Allowance (DLA), is not covered by the DDA unless she is considered disabled under the Act. The problem lies with the definition of disability, in that it focuses on individuals' impairment/s rather than on the level and nature of resultant discrimination. This reflects a medical model of disability which holds that impairment is responsible for limited opportunities, not discriminatory practice. Fortunately, it may be that things are set to improve. The Disability Rights Commission (DRC) is currently (at the time of writing) engaged in public consultation on the definition of disability in anti-discrimination law, proposing that attention be shifted away from particular conditions to whether discrimination is occurring. The long-term aim is that any change to the definition will feed in to a new Single Equalities Act, which the government is looking to produce by 2010. Current thinking is that the new Act should embrace six dimensions of equality: religion, race, gender, age, sexuality and disability.

Full-time inclusive educational provision for children with medical conditions

Nowadays, most children with medical conditions are able to attend mainstream school regularly and, with appropriate support from practitioners, can take part in most activities. Indeed, the vast majority of children with medical conditions attend mainstream school. Some attend special schools, however, where their needs are severe and complex or cannot be met within mainstream settings without compromising others' education, or because parents have expressed a preference for their child to attend a special school.

In the interest of countering the negative effects of segregation, some special schools run link schemes whereby children attend their local mainstream school for a stated number of hours each week, accompanied by a teacher or teaching assistant, so that they may build social relationships with their peers. While such schemes do promote social relationships, they are somewhat difficult to maintain and do not necessarily support inclusive education (Sebba and Sachdev 1997).

Prior to the advent of special schools in the 1950s, it was accepted that children with chronic or serious illness would simply not attend school. Special schools were developed to provide education for children with disability and/or SEN, which naturally included some children with medical conditions. The late 1970s, however, saw the beginning of a shift away from the segregation of children with SEN and/or disabilities from mainstream educational provision. In 1978, the Warnock Report announced that all children, regardless of their particular needs or disabilities, should be educated alongside their peers in mainstream classrooms (Warnock 1978). Three years later, the Education Act 1981 facilitated the move towards the inclusion of children, who might otherwise have been educated in special schools or 'remedial' classrooms in mainstream schools.

The ideology of inclusive education pre-dates the Warnock Report by some considerable number of years; indeed, it can be traced back to the beginning of the twentieth century (O'Brien and Forest 1989). Having said this, however, the emergence of contemporary inclusive education in the UK is very much rooted in the Warnock Report and has since gathered momentum following the Conference on Special Education which took place in Salamanca, Spain in 1994. The Salamanca Statement, signed by 92 governments, including the UK, and 25 international organizations, reflecting widespread commitment to the ethos of inclusive education, proclaims that inclusive education must become the norm for all disabled children. The Salamanca Conference espoused a new 'Framework for Action', the guiding principle of which is that 'regular' schools should accommodate all children, regardless of 'individual differences' (UNESCO 1994).

Present-day government policy, notably, *Removing Barriers to Achievement* (DfES 2004a), reflects New Labour's commitment to inclusive education and has engendered even more emphasis on the benefits to children of joining their peers in mainstream settings.

Inclusive education can be defined as 'a process involving changes in the way schools are organized, in the curriculum and in teaching strategies, to accommodate the range of needs and abilities among pupils' (Sebba and Sachdev 1997: 2). Thus it can be seen to represent more than integration. The reality, however, is different in that segregation occurs within mainstream settings for many children. Children supported by one-to-one learning support workers, for example, are frequently separated from their peers. Others are prevented from enjoying the same activities as their peers due to the absence of requisite support mechanisms within settings. Thus, it can be seen that in many instances attendance at mainstream is tantamount to exclusion. Insufficient funding, limited resources and lack of expertise present huge barriers to the successful inclusion of children with complex needs. It is important, however, to note that things are not all bad; many children fare better both academically and socially in mainstream classrooms. Indeed, there exists research to support this claim (Sebba and Sachdev 1997).

Access to successful inclusive education should be the right of all children, not just some. We have an education system, however, that is failing a substantial number of children with SEN/disabilities in mainstream schools, whilst also placing huge demands on staff in terms of supporting these children (House of Commons Education and Skills Committee 2006).

Inclusive education, ever since its formal introduction in the late 1970s, has been the subject of much debate. Currently, proponents of wholesale inclusion such as the Centre for Studies on Inclusive Education (CSIE) and a number of adults who attended special schools as children and who now call themselves 'special school survivors', argue for wholesale inclusion as a basic human right and recommend the closure of all special schools and far greater investment in supporting mainstream settings in achieving successful inclusion. The government, however, sees a clear ongoing role for special schools as centres of excellence for specific types of need and as direct providers for children with highly complex needs. Others, including Baroness Warnock and the National Association of Head Teachers, argue that successful inclusive education is dependent on combining mainstream and special school provision, asserting that wholesale inclusion fails to meet the needs of a significant number of children, especially those with behavioural and emotional problems and children with autism (National Association of Head Teachers 2003, Warnock 2005).

As well as proposing a shift away from wholesale inclusion, Warnock (2005) recommends a radical change to the function of statements of SEN, declaring that statements would be more useful as 'passports' to attendance at special schools and that SEN should only be catered for in mainstream where this can be supported by settings' own resources without additional support from the LA. These suggestions have, however, been put forward in the absence of consultation with children with SEN and/or disability and their families.

Like Warnock (2005), the DRC want to revisit inclusion policy, but in consultation with those who have day-to-day experience of the current system. Others, including the House of Commons Education and Skills Select Committee (2006) and Ofsted (2004), for example, have also called for a review of current educational provision for children with SEN and/or disability in light of some 'serious flaws' in the current system with regard to standards and consistency of provision, the statementing process, fair access to settings and outcomes for children with SEN and disability.

Activity

Update and enhance your knowledge of issues relevant to inclusive education. The Centre for Studies on Inclusive Education (CSIE: http:// inclusion.uwe.ac.uk/csie) provides a very useful starting point. See also, Warnock, M. (2005) *Special Educational Needs: A New Look, Impact No.11,* London, Philosophy of Education. Another extremely useful source of information is part of the Barnardos 'What Works' series: *What Works in Inclusive Education,* by Judy Shedda and Darshan Sachdev. This can be obtained from the Barnardos website at: www.barnardos.org.uk/resources. See also the House of Commons Education and Skills Select Committee report on the inquiry into SEN provision, published July 2006.

There follows an extreme case, taken from the Disability Rights Commission website (www.drc.org.uk), of a school's failure to adequately support, and therefore include, a child with SEN. The case description does not indicate whether or not the child has a medical condition but he may well have. The name of the school is not identified here and a pseudonym is used to refer to the child.

Case example: Matthew, 6 years

Matthew, who has learning disabilities, was left out of the school Christmas play even though all his classmates were taking part. He had to stay behind

---

in the classroom whilst his schoolmates went to rehearsals.

Matthew was also not allowed to take part in any of the other school's Christmas activities; including making the scenery for the Christmas play, making decorations, and he was not invited to the school Christmas disco. He was the only child in his class not to bring home a homemade Christmas card.

However, this was the tip of the iceberg. Matthew had a statement of SEN, and the school was given funding for a full-time Learning Support Assistant. For most of the time that Matthew attended the school, it failed to appoint a suitable full-time support worker. This meant that Matthew could only join in class for two hours a day when his support worker was there. As a consequence, Matthew was often timetabled to spend most of his time at school on his own, away from the other children, either with his mother or with an inexperienced Learning Support Assistant. His mother has calculated that Matthew has lost 920 hours of support. The lack of support had a huge impact on Matthew and his mother.

He was often excluded from many other school activities, including assembly, singing, computers, numeracy and literacy work. At one stage, when there was no support worker at all, Matthew's mother had to come to school with him every day.

On the occasion that the class photographs were taken, Matthew was not asked to come into school to join in the photograph. The photo was subsequently displayed in the school. Every child except Matthew was in the photograph. Matthew often returned to the photo and could not understand why he was not included.

In October 2003, Matthew's mother took the school to the SEN Tribunal (SENDIST). His case was supported by the Disability Rights Commission (DRC). The Tribunal upheld that the school discriminated against Matthew by treating him 'less favourably' because of his disability and that the school failed to adopt a practice of recruiting or retaining support staff for Matthew. This said the Tribunal, 'does amount to discrimination' and ordered the school to apologize in writing to Matthew and his mother.

The school has also been ordered to prepare or revise all the schools' policies for their disabled pupils and for recruiting and retaining staff. The governing body and all staff must also attend disability equality training.

According to the DRC, the child in question is now happily attending another school.

Discussion/reflection

♦ Consider the impact of the school's failings on Matthew's emotional development; particularly his sense of self-worth.

♦ Consider the impact on Matthew's relationship with his peers.

> ◆ Think about the effects of being witness to such discriminatory practice on Matthew's classmates.
>
> ◆ Imagine what it must have felt like for Matthew's parents to see their son being discriminated against in this way.
>
> ◆ The case highlights some of the reasons for the schools failings; what are they? Can you think of some other possible contributory factors?

Formal education outside school

While every endeavour is made to educate children with medical conditions within mainstream class-rooms – even where such needs are complex – illness or injury can sometimes result in a need for education to be provided outside school. This may be on a short or a long-term basis, or it may be an intermittent need. A child may be unable to attend school due to the need for hospitalization, for example, or she may feel too ill to go to school. She may have mental health issues that preclude her attendance at school, or her symptoms may be such that her attendance at school poses a health and safety risk to others.

Section 19 of the Education Act 1996, as amended by Section 47 of the Education Act 1997, places a duty on LAs to provide 'suitable' education for children outside school. Every year in the UK, approximately 100,000 children have need of such education because of illness (short and long-term) or injury (DfES 2001b). Suitable out-of-school education refers to education that is tailored to meet the needs of each individual child and is adaptable to the demands of changing needs.

Out-of-school education can be provided via hospital schools or hospital teaching, home-teaching, an integrated hospital/home education service or pupil referral unit, depending on the needs of the child and the availability of services in the child's area of residence.

A hospital school, as its name suggests, is a special school, maintained by the LA, operated within a hospital setting. Hospital schools provide education to in-patients in the main; however, some children with chronic illness attend daily from home. Hospital schools are self-directed and manage their own budgets, and do not have a legislative duty to offer the National Curriculum. Home-teaching refers to one-to-one education delivered in a child's home environment and should be available to all who need it. Home-teaching is often combined with education delivered within a hospital setting.

A pupil referral unit is both a school in its own right and a source of out-of-school education. Established and maintained by the LA, pupil referral units provide education for school-age children who, as a result of illness or exclusion from school, would otherwise be unable to access appropriate education. Education in a pupil referral unit is seen as a short-term measure. Children are admitted with clear targets for reintegration into mainstream or special schooling.

Whatever the mode of provision, ultimate aims must be to ensure continuity of educational provision, through effective liaison between hospital, home, pupil referral units and school, and successful reintegration into mainstream provision when a child no longer requires out-of-school education (supporting reintegration will be discussed in Chapter 5).

For more information on provision of education outside school, see *Access to Education for Children and Young People with Medical Needs* (DfES 2001b).

Supporting inclusion in pre-school settings

The following organizations, between them, provide a wealth of information and resources for practitioners working towards the successful inclusion of children with medical conditions in pre-school settings:

◆ Pre-school Learning Alliance – supports practitioners and staff working in pre-school settings in developing inclusive practice. The alliance is committed to the inclusion of young children with SEN and impairments in early years settings.

◆ Disability Equality in Education – has produced a teaching pack aimed at developing an understanding of disability and promoting inclusion in the early years, called 'All equal, all different'. The pack is available from their website (below).

◆ The Centre for Studies on Inclusive Education – has produced a detailed set of materials to help support early years and childcare settings to increase the participation of all young children in learning and play, namely, 'Index for inclusion – developing learning, participation and play in early years and childcare' (available from the CSIE website, below).

◆ Scope for Parents – supports the inclusion of disabled children in early years settings.

Useful contacts

Action for Sick Children
Telephone: 020 7843 6444
Website: www.actionforsickchildren.org

Alliance for Inclusive Education
Telephone: 020 7735 5277

Centre for Studies on Inclusive Education
Telephone: 0117 328 4007
Website: http://inclusion.uwe.ac.uk/csie/csiehome.htm

Council for Disabled Children
Telephone: 020 7843 6000
Website: www.ncb.org.uk

Disability Equality in Education
Telephone: 020 7359 2855
Website: www.diseed.org.uk

National Association for the Education of Sick Children
Telephone: 020 8980 8523
Website: www.sickchildren.org.uk

Pre-school Learning Alliance
Telephone: 020 7697 2500

Scope for Parents
Website: www.scope.org.uk

2

Growing Up with a Medical Condition

Although the experience of a medical condition can vary widely from one condition to another, children with medical conditions are probably as similar as they are different (Vessey and Mebane 2000). As such, discussion within this chapter will focus on children's experience of having a medical condition per se as opposed to the effects of individual conditions. The chapter will consider the impact of a medical condition on a child's development according to developmental stage and will examine how stressors, sometimes associated with living with a medical condition, can impact on children's behavioural, social and emotional development.

Learning outcomes

When you have read this chapter, you should be able to:

♦ Understand some of the effects of having a medical condition on daily living

♦ Describe ways in which medical conditions can impact on child development and explain the difference between a direct and indirect effect

♦ Recognize that many children with medical conditions face a myriad of day-to-day stressors that can have an adverse effect on their behavioural, social and emotional development, and briefly explain what is meant by risk and resilience factors in this context

Long-term medical conditions

This section considers some general issues concerning medical conditions affecting children, including: prevalence and co-morbidity (two or more diseases existing together in a person), living with a medical condition and different levels of severity. Discussion relevant to the actual disease process, however, including the aetiology (cause) and the signs and symptoms of a vast number of possible conditions, is not deemed appropriate. For one thing, this would require a book in itself, and a very large one at that. Indeed, such information is readily available in books, journals, government guidance and on websites developed and maintained by national organizations supporting people with specific conditions, such as Asthma UK, Diabetes UK, Contact a Family, and so on (see the list of useful contacts at the end of this chapter). From hereon in, the terms long-term illness, chronic illness, medical condition and chronic medical condition will be used interchangeably to denote conditions such as the following:

♦ Asthma (the most common condition affecting children)

Medical Conditions

◆ Diabetes

◆ Epilepsy

◆ Anaphylaxis

◆ Attention Deficit Hyperactivity Disorder (ADHD)

◆ Cancer and leukaemia

◆ Cystic fibrosis

◆ Cerebral palsy

◆ HIV/AIDS

◆ Skin conditions (e.g. eczema and psoriasis)

◆ Rheumatoid arthritis

◆ Psychosomatic disorders such as Chronic Fatigue Syndrome

◆ Emotional disorders such as anxiety, phobia and depression

◆ Traumatic brain injury

◆ Cardiovascular conditions

◆ Haemophilia

Activity

◆ Collate as much information as you can about a medical condition affecting a child in your setting.

◆ Decide where you will obtain the information from, e.g. books, journals, reliable websites, a health professional.

◆ Find out, if you can, the incidence of the condition. This information is usually, but not always, available.

◆ Is there a known cause?

◆ Find out how the condition primarily affects the body, e.g. asthma causes inflammation of the airways.

◆ Is there a specific age of onset?

◆ What are the symptoms?

◆ What treatment options are available and are there any side-effects?

◆ Make sure this information is available to all personnel and is regularly updated.

Again, this list is used purely for illustrative purposes and is by no means comprehensive.

The more you know about a medical condition affecting a child, the better equipped you will be to support that child and to empathize with him. In fact, it is imperative that everyone caring for and educating young children with medical conditions develop sound knowledge and understanding of conditions affecting children for whom they have responsibility.

In 1995, the British Paediatric Association (BPA)

estimated that ten per cent of children under 15 have an illness which chronically impedes their ability to function (BPA 1995). This estimate does not include short-term illness. These children may suffer from one or a combination of two or possibly more of the conditions listed above. On the other hand, they may be diagnosed with a somewhat rare medical condition and, in some instances, have another more common long-term illness as well. Some children with chronic physical illness will have a co-morbid psychiatric disorder.

Living with a medical condition may involve ongoing or intermittent pain and/or discomfort, ongoing or episodic fatigue, having to undergo distressing procedures, missing out on normal day-to-day activities, being separated from family and peers during periods of hospitalization, feeling different and being disfigured, disabled and/or fatally ill. Although some of these factors are not unique to children with medical conditions, they are likely to manifest more frequently and with greater severity, last longer and to overlap in these children.

Reflection

Try to imagine what it must be like to suffer a severe bout of eczema involving incessant itchiness, day and night. If you have ever endured an episode of non-stop itchiness, think back to how unpleasant it was. This will help you to reflect on what it would be like to suffer such discomfort for days on end. Imagine trying to work or get things done around the house whilst being irritated to the point of utter distraction by constantly itchy skin. Imagine scratching yourself so furiously that you make yourself bleed. Try to conceive of what it must be like to concentrate in the face of ongoing sleep deprivation brought about by relentless itchiness. Imagine how utterly exhausted such sleep deprivation would make you feel, and how it would affect your mood. Lack of sleep certainly makes for a short fuse in most people, including children. How would you feel at the outset of an exacerbation, having been free of irritation for weeks and knowing what is in store for you? Depressed, I would imagine. Have you ever had some sort of blemish on your face that made you feel self-conscious? Imagine your skin covered in sore red patches.

It is important for practitioners and everyone caring for a child with a medical condition to reflect, every now and again, on what it must be like to live with that particular condition. It is easy to forget sometimes, especially when a child seems accepting of a condition, the extent to which his life may be affected by it.

Our understanding of what it is like to grow up with a chronic illness is based to a very large extent on parents' perceptions of how their child is affected. Thus it could be said that our understanding is somewhat limited, given that, as parents we often overestimate how much we understand our children's feelings (Eiser 2000). Moreover, where parents are distressed by their child's illness, they are even less likely to provide precise representation of their child's day-to-day experience of a medical condition and have a tendency to overreport difficulties. Where parents are seriously depressed, for example, there is evidence to suggest that they report more behaviour problems in their child. Despite some initial misgivings, the consensus nowadays is that it is children themselves who are best placed to provide accurate and reliable accounts of what it is like to live and grow up with a chronic medical condition (Eiser 2000).

The severity with which children are affected varies both across and within conditions. In other words, some conditions are more severe than others, in terms of their effects on the child, and certain conditions vary themselves in the extent to which they affect children. Asthma, for instance, while causing some children very little disruption to daily living, can severely disable others. Some conditions are stable, whilst others may change for better or worse. Such change can be long-term – an example being a child who grows out of asthma – or cyclical. Cyclical change refers to relapses and remissions, characteristic of conditions such as leukaemia.

Medical conditions and child development

In addition to enduring intermittent or persistent symptoms, and the unpleasant side-effects of medication and/or invasive and often painful medical procedures, some children with chronic medical conditions face delay or difficulties in relation to their developmental progress. This section will examine the impact on a child's developmental progress of having a medical condition. It will also highlight some of the stressors that chronically ill children must face and how these stressors can potentially compromise their social, emotional and behavioural development and well-being.

The negative impact of a medical condition on a child's development can be direct or indirect. The impact is direct if the illness itself affects some aspect of a child's functioning; for example, an illness that causes damage to the brain causing impaired cognitive functioning. Indeed, direct effects are most likely where conditions affect the brain or other parts of the nervous system. Examples include: infections such as encephalitis and meningitis; metabolic disorders such as hypothyroidism; inherited degenerative conditions such as tuberous sclerosis, and other degenerative diseases, such as Auto Immune Deficiency Syndrome (AIDS). Epilepsy, a disorder of the brain itself, can also have a direct effect on a child's development where it is so severe as to impair cognitive functioning.

The impact of a medical condition on development is indirect when secondary factors inhibit the achievement of developmental tasks; for example, frequent or prolonged absence from school or chronic fatigue may hinder a child's learning. Chronically ill children can develop secondary internalizing and acting out of behaviour problems in instances where living with a medical condition is particularly stressful. This too can have a negative impact on a child's ability to learn. Finally, some children require treatment that can adversely affect development. A child with acute lymphoblastic leukaemia, for example, may need cranial radiation which, whilst greatly reducing the risk of relapse, can have adverse effects on cognitive functioning.

Impact according to developmental stage

Each developmental stage gives rise to particular challenges for children with medical conditions. During infancy, for example, being subjected to painful medical procedures may compromise a child's ability to build trusting relationships with adults. Toddlers may be prevented from acquiring independence in tasks such as toileting and feeding. Pre-school age children, who are immuno-supressed, for example, will very likely be unable to take advantage of opportunities such as attending pre-school, an activity proven to enhance cognitive functioning. For school-age children, lack of energy might preclude participation in school activities designed to contribute to the acquiring of social skills.

Infancy (0–12 months)

Infancy is a time when children should be building their trust in adults. Children with medical conditions, however, may experience, through hospitalization, frequent or possibly long periods of separation from their parents, as well as exposure to numerous caregivers. Although, nowadays, parents are encouraged to stay with and care for their child in hospital and, indeed, provision is made for this, not all parents are able to do so, especially those who have other children at home requiring care and supervision (Eiser 2000). Frequent and/or prolonged separation, and the uncertainty associated with numerous caregivers for older infants, have the potential to impede secure attachment and the development of trusting relationships in this age group.

Parents vary in how they respond to and cope with chronic illness affecting their child. Some cope remarkably well while others, for any number of reasons, find coping with and coming to terms with the situation very difficult indeed. Some parents 'mourn the loss of their perfect child' and may thereby lack the requisite enthusiasm and drive to respond adequately to their child's needs (Vessey and Mebane 2000: 22). Conversely, others are overprotective and outwardly anxious. A poor prognosis may cause some parents to distance themselves from their child in an attempt to shield against further emotional pain. All these factors can inhibit the development of secure attachment.

Case example: Darren, 3 years

Darren was born at 29 weeks gestation. He spent the first three months of his life in hospital. During the initial few weeks of his life, Darren's condition was very unstable and his prognosis difficult to predict. He was discharged home at 36 weeks, but developed further respiratory complications so had to be readmitted. He was successfully discharged home at 38 weeks, his prognosis optimistic by then. Darren's parents lost their first baby, Emma, to sudden infant death syndrome at the age of 5 months. While Darren was in hospital, his mother visited him every day initially, although sometimes she would only stay a couple of hours or so. As time went by, however, her visits became fewer and further between. Darren's father visited him as often as he possibly could within the constraints of

---

working full-time. Darren's parents separated when he was 8 months old (chronological age) and, soon after, his mother developed severe depression. While her illness was at its worst, members of her extended family pulled together and took it in turns to care for Darren in order to afford her some respite. Darren was a very irritable infant; difficult to console. As a toddler he was shy and fearful. He attends play school now where there is concern over his quiet, cautious and withdrawn demeanour.

As already mentioned, children with chronic medical conditions may be subjected to invasive and often unpleasant and painful medical procedures by adults. For the infant, the reasons for these cannot be explained, given their young age. As such, these 'physical assaults' may constitute another threat to the infant's ability to build trusting relationships with adults (Eiser 2000: 28). Very young infants, however, are an exception in that they lack the requisite level of cognition to attribute such 'physical assaults' to, as yet, incompletely differentiated important caregivers (Barker 1993).

In addition, global developmental delay can occur in very early childhood where long-term illness causes chronic fatigue and/or pain rendering the infant incapable of learning about his environment through motor sensor exploration.

Toddlerhood (12–36 months)

As a child moves through toddlerhood, major developmental tasks include the development of autonomy and self-control and the acquisition of speech and language. Children in this age group therefore require exposure to social environments rich in opportunities to develop these skills. Toddlers with medical conditions, however, are often inhibited from taking advantage of such opportunities due to the nature of their symptoms and/or the need for some form of restriction, for example, the need to limit social contacts where a child is susceptible to, and could be severely compromised by, infection.

Compared to other age groups, toddlers experiencing acute exacerbations of chronic illness or a serious condition are particularly vulnerable to behavioural regression whereby recently mastered developmental tasks are temporarily lost. Behavioural regression is believed by some to be the result of insufficient 'psychic energy' to maintain functioning at developmental levels already achieved (Freud 1966).

Case example: Lee, 18 months

At the age of 14 months, Lee was diagnosed with infantile fibrosarcoma of the thigh. He had to undergo two operations to remove the lesion. He also had a course of radiotherapy. The paediatric oncologist recently reassured Lee's parents that she is happy with his progress, but will continue to monitor him for the time being. Lee's parents are worried, however, with regard to his apparent

---

disinterest in trying to walk, whereas, prior to his illness, he had taken a few steps on his own. They are also concerned about his speech development as this appears to have regressed. The paediatrician feels that this behavioural regression is probably no more than a normal response to illness in this age group. However, she has referred him for specialist assessment and advice on management.

Pre-school age children (3–5 years)

Developmental theorists, including Piaget, Vygotsky, Erickson and others, have taught us that pre-school children thrive on daily routines that encourage the development of independence, competence and autonomy; facilitate practice of new skills, especially through the imitation of others; and enable them to learn, through interaction with others, the minutiae of social norms. Pre-school age children need also to develop fine motor skills and build muscle control. Some medical conditions can compromise the achievement of all of these skills (Eiser 2000). Moreover, this age group is particularly vulnerable to the effects of intermittent or prolonged separation from their main caregivers (Eiser 2000). A seminal study into the effects of hospitalization found that a significant number of children experienced negative reactions following discharge which, in over 50 per cent of children, persisted for several months (Prugh et al. 1953). Subsequent studies have also reported post-hospitalization problems affecting this age group (e.g. Brain and Maclay 1968, Goslin 1979, Rossen and McKeever 1996), including: night terrors, irritability, feeding problems, behavioural regression and separation anxiety, especially intolerance of separation from the mother.

Case example: Nathan, 3 years, 3 months

Nathan contracted bacterial meningitis just prior to his third birthday. He was very ill indeed and was hospitalized for nine days. Fortunately, however, he did not suffer any long-term complications other than mild hearing loss. Prior to becoming ill, Nathan attended play school regularly, which he enjoyed. His parents are very keen for him to resume attending but, to date, he has not been up to it due to suffering minor illness after minor illness. Susceptibility to illness is common following meningitis. Much as Nathan's parents are anxious for him to return to play school, their main concern is the change in his character since coming home from hospital. He has become very clingy and given to frequent and explosive temper tantrums. He also seems unable to entertain himself for even short periods of time. Instead he constantly demands attention from his parents. Another worry is that, having been dry at night since the age of two and a half, Nathan has started wetting the bed. His parents have decided to contact their health visitor for advice on these issues.

The nature and degree of the effects of being in hospital depends not only on a child's age, but also on his personality and past experiences and what happens to him in hospital. An only child, who spends much of his time at home with his main caregiver, is wary of strangers and has already been exposed to traumatic separation from his parents, is at increased risk of developing some of the emotional effects listed above. Negative post-hospitalization reactions are also more common in children who have undergone surgery or some other procedure requiring general anaesthetic. Current policy, relevant to the needs of children in hospital and their families (see Chapter 4), places huge emphasis on normalizing, as far as is possible, a child's experience of hospital with the aim of minimizing the potential for negative reactions following discharge. It is acknowledged that this can only be achieved through holistic child and family centred care, delivered in an environment that is appropriate to a child's age and stage of development.

School-age children

School-age children with chronic medical conditions are particularly vulnerable to behavioural and emotional difficulties. Eiser (1990: 85) concluded that the 'weight of scientific evidence continues to point to increased vulnerability in terms of emotional and behavioural development'. More recent studies support this assertion (e.g. McDermott *et al.* 1996). Problems include the emotional effects of separation and hospitalization; depressive symptoms; anxiety and acting out and internalizing behaviour problems. For young children the emotional effects of separation from parents and other aspects of hospitalization are compounded by the fact that they attribute their illness to something they have done wrong, as though it were some sort of punishment for disobedience, for example (Perrin and Gerrity 1981). On a positive note, researchers emphasize that only a small minority of children with long-term illness experience the above problems and that attribution of self-blame decreases with age (Eiser 1990, Perrin and Gerrity 1981).

Wolff (1981: 66–7) provides a moving illustration of attribution of self-blame in a child (Mark) for the occurrence of illness. She describes her involvement in getting to the bottom of why Mark, having stoically endured weeks of immobilization in plaster, develops food refusal and vomiting on being moved to a convalescent home, and outlines the steps that were taken to decrease his sense of responsibility for his illness. The case makes very interesting and informative reading.

Wolff (1981) asserts that children between the ages of three and seven years are more likely to attribute their illness to something they have done and that they are therefore dependent on adults to help them make sense of their illness. Current policy (see Chapter 4) reflects this assertion in that it recommends that children who are ill should be given information, by adults responsible for their care, about their condition and associated procedures and that explanation should be tailored to each individual child's level of understanding and conveyed using 'child-friendly' language.

Stressors

Although the potential impact of a medical condition on a child's behaviour, social and emotional development has been mentioned frequently within the previous section, it is felt that this issue also merits at least a short section of its own. As such, this section examines the effect of stressors (part and parcel of living with a long-term illness) on these aspects of child development. The following home and school-setting stressors are likely to affect the behavioural social and emotional development of children with medical conditions:

◆ Understanding the diagnosis, prognosis and treatment

◆ Adapting to treatment and side-effects

◆ Relating to medical staff

◆ Relating to family and peers

◆ Dealing with two worlds, illness and health; 'being special' and 'being ordinary'

(Eiser 2000: 34)

It has been asserted that medical conditions 'should be conceptualized as one of the most important early risk factors for emotional disturbance' (Barker 1993: 82). It must be noted, however, that although children with chronic conditions constitute a group susceptible to behavioural and emotional problems, this is not the most common outcome (Eiser 1990).

Unfortunately, there exists a dearth of research into the long-term psychological development of children who do experience such problems. Much more longitudinal research is needed into the long-term effects, including impact on adulthood of emotional difficulties secondary to long-term illness during childhood. Research in this field is complicated, however due to changes in physical status over time and, where comparison groups are used, well children acquiring a chronic condition (Wallander and Varni 1998).

Whether or not emotional, social and behavioural problems do ensue in children with medical conditions, and their severity, depends on a number of factors, including: how much support the child receives; the child's cognitive understanding of illness; the child's age; the prognosis of the illness; and the extent of resilience in the child.

It is imperative that children receive support in dealing with chronic illness-related stress, be it from family, health professionals, early years practitioners and/or peers. Support from peers is particularly beneficial. Varni *et al.* (1994) found that perceived support from peers, classmates in this instance, significantly reduced depressive symptoms, anxiety states and behaviour problems, as well as raising children's self-esteem. For many school-age children with medical conditions, however, absence makes it difficult for them to build and sustain relationships with peers, leading to feelings of isolation (Bolton 1997). Moreover, contact with friends is limited for those children who have no option but to spend break times having treatment or on personal care tasks (Lightfoot *et al.* 1998). Sadly, a significant number of children with medical conditions experience anything but support from peers. Instead, they face frequent bombardment of questions about their condition stemming from peer curiosity or worse, they are bullied because of seeming or looking different from other children (Lightfoot *et al.* 1998).

Discussion in Chapter 5 is concerned with supporting children with medical conditions in early years settings, including how early years practitioners can engender empathy and support in other children towards those with chronic illness.

Greater cognitive development appears to be linked to a better ability to cope with the effects of chronic illness and associated procedures. Thus the young child, apart from the very young infant, with a medical condition is more likely to suffer ensuing emotional and behaviour problems than his older counterparts. Also, a child with normal, for developmental stage, cognitive functioning, is less likely to suffer emotional stress than a child with mild to moderate learning difficulties.

Wallander and Varni (1998) have identified amendable 'risk and resistance factors' relevant to the development or otherwise of social, emotional and behaviour problems in children with medical conditions (pp. 31–7). The authors offer heuristic (learning through investigation) guidance on developing strategies for supporting children with chronic medical conditions. These encapsulate the impact of illness prognosis and resilience factors in the child on psychological well-being in the face of chronic illness, as well as the effects of cognitive functioning and level of support, whether the latter is actual or perceived.

Risk factors

♦ Disease/disability parameters (e.g. diagnosis, 'handicap' severity, medical complications, bowel/bladder control, visibility, cognitive functioning, brain impairment)

♦ Functional dependence in the activities of daily living

♦ Psychosocial stressors (disability-related problems, major life events, daily hassles)

Resistance factors

♦ Intrapersonal factors such as competence, temperament, motivation and problem-solving ability

♦ Social-ecological factors such as family psychological environment, social support, family members' adaptation and practical resources available to the family

♦ Stress-processing factors such as cognitive appraisal and coping strategies

(Wallander and Varni 1998: 31)

Activity

Find out more about 'risk and resistance factors'. This will enable you to take the necessary steps to reduce, as far as possible, risk factors for social, emotional and behavioural problems in children with medical conditions, and also to enhance children's resilience quotient. Read the Wallander and Varni (1998) article where these factors are explored in depth and in the light of clinically relevant research. Try to find more up-to-date work around risk and resilience factors. You could do a 'Health and Social Care' academic database search if you have access to the necessary facilities and are proficient in this activity. If not, you may have a friend or colleague who could do this for you or you could try finding relevant information through a search engine such as Google. Should you decide on the latter, you would have to be certain that you act only on information obtained from reliable sources. Wallander and Varni (1998) noted that awareness of risk and resilience offers 'heuristic guidance'; therefore, if you work in an early years setting and decide to employ a new strategy aimed at reducing risk or enhancing resistance, then the intervention must of course be evidenced-based and its impact in the setting evaluated.

Useful contacts

Allergy UK
Telephone: 01322 619 864
Website: www.allergyfoundation.com

Association for Spina Bifida and Hydrocephalus
Telephone: 01733 555 988
Website: www.asbah.org

Asthma UK
Telephone: 08457 01 02 03
Website: www.asthma.org.uk

Contact a Family
Telephone: 0808 808 3555
Website: www.cafamily.org.uk

Cystic Fibrosis Trust
Telephone: 020 8464 7211
Website: www.cftrust.org.uk

Diabetes UK
Telephone: 0845 120 2960

Mencap
Telephone: 020 7454 0454
Website: www.mencap.org.uk

National Eczema Association
Telephone: 0870 241 3604
Website: www.eczema.org

Psoriasis Association
Telephone: 0845 676 0076
Website: www.psoriasis-association.org.uk

3

Medical Conditions with Associated SEN

In this chapter readers will be reminded of the potential overlap between medical needs, SEN and disability. The legal definition of SEN will be considered, followed by discussion around recognizing SEN in children with medical conditions. Comprehensive discussion relevant to SEN processes and procedures will then ensue.

Learning outcomes

When you have read this chapter, you should be able to:

♦ Differentiate between difficulty in learning and SEN

♦ Describe some of the difficulties associated with recognizing SEN in children with medical conditions

♦ Outline the graduated response to SEN

♦ Appreciate some of the difficulties associated with the current SEN system

♦ Describe the support options available to children with medical conditions exposed to SEN processes and procedures, and their families

It is important to summarize at this juncture, some pertinent points regarding the overlap between medical conditions and SEN. To recap, some children with medical conditions do not have associated SEN or disability; some have a medical condition and SEN; whereas others have a medical condition, SEN and disability (see Figure 1.1 p. 7). You may recall that children with a medical condition and/or disability are only regarded as having SEN where a medical condition affects their learning capacity, and that this can be a direct or an indirect effect. A direct effect occurs where a condition affects the brain or another part of the nervous system or is a disorder of the brain itself; whereas an indirect effect on learning happens when secondary factors such as intermittent and/or prolonged absence from an educational setting or chronic fatigue, for example, impede learning. In essence, where there is evidence that a medical condition may compromise, or is compromising, a child's ability to learn, then she has SEN (and might also have a disability) and her education must therefore be underpinned by the fundamental principles relevant to the education of children with SEN, as set out in the SEN Code of Practice (DfES 2001a):

♦ Children with special educational needs should have their needs met;

♦ The special educational needs of children will normally be met in mainstream schools or settings;

Medical Conditions

♦ The views of the child should be sought and taken into account;

♦ Parents have a vital role to play in supporting their child's education;

♦ Children with special educational needs should be offered full access to a broad, balanced and relevant education, including an appropriate curriculum for the foundation stage and the National Curriculum.

(DfES 2001a: 7)

Based on the 1996 Education Act, the SEN Code of Practice defines SEN as follows:

Children have special educational needs if they have a *learning difficulty* which calls for *special educational provision* to be made for them.

Children have a *learning difficulty* if they:

a) have significantly greater difficulty in learning than the majority of children the same age;

b) have a disability which prevents or hinders them from making use of educational facilities of a kind generally provided for children of the same age in schools within the area of the local authority;

c) are under compulsory school age and fall within the definition at a) or b) above or would do so if special educational provision was not made for them.

(DfES 2001a: 6, based on Section 312 of the Education Act 1996)

With regard to point (a), children who have greater difficulty in learning than their peers, either generally or in relation to a specific area of learning, do not necessarily have SEN (note that the definition refers to 'significantly greater difficulty'). Progress is measured against government targets relevant to what children should be able to do according to certain ages. These are the Early Learning Goals of the Foundation Stage for three to five year olds and the Attainment Targets of the National Curriculum for five to sixteen year olds. Point (b) naturally includes some children with medical conditions.

Special educational provision means:

a) for children of two or over, educational provision which is additional to, or otherwise different from, the educational provision made generally for children of their age in schools maintained by the LA, other than special schools, in the area.
b) for children under two, educational provision of any kind.

> (DfES 2001a: 6, based on Section 312. of the Education Act 1996)

Children found to be making slow educational progress require 'carefully differentiated learning opportunities' (DfES 2001a: 33), aimed at expediting their learning, together with regular and frequent monitoring to ensure adequate progress is being made.

Adequate progress can be defined as progress that:

◆ Closes the attainment gap between the child and the child's peers

- ◆ Prevents the attainment gap growing wider

- ◆ Is similar to that of peers starting from the same attainment baseline, but less than that of the majority of peers

- ◆ Matches or betters the child's previous rate of progress

- ◆ Ensures access to the full curriculum

- ◆ Demonstrates an improvement in self-help, social or personal skills

- ◆ Demonstrates improvements in behaviour
(DfES, 2001a:34)

In the event of inadequate progress, then it must be assumed that a child has SEN and therefore requires educational provision above that which is generally available in schools and early years settings.

Specific difficulties

Children under five with SEN may have difficulties in one or more of the following areas:

- ◆ Communication

- ◆ Understanding and learning

- ◆ Sensory and physical development

- ◆ Behaviour or relating to other people
(www.directgov.uk)

School-age children with SEN may have similar difficulties, as well as difficulties surrounding formal education. They may encounter problems in one or more of the following areas:

♦ School work

♦ Reading, writing, number work or understanding information

♦ Expressing themselves or understanding what others are saying

♦ Making friends or relating to adults

♦ Behaving properly in school

♦ Organizing themselves

♦ Some kind of sensory or physical needs which may affect them in school

(www.directgov.uk)

Recognizing SEN in children with medical conditions

As already mentioned in the first chapter, some children with medical conditions may have SEN which go unrecognized, simply because their condition does not have an obvious effect on their physical or cognitive functioning. Closs (2005) asserts that misinterpretation of 'learning difficulty' by professionals often gives rise to such confusion. This she says is because 'learning difficulty' is frequently assumed to refer to 'some degree of cognitive impairment resulting in globally and constantly lowered performance' (p. 5). Such an assumption is set to preclude a number of children with medical conditions from accessing additional educational provision that would benefit their education (Closs 2000). This situation could be ameliorated by making absolutely certain that children with medical conditions whose educational progress is slower than that of their peers benefit from 'carefully differentiated learning opportunities' and careful monitoring (DfES 2001a: 33). What of the child, though, whose medical condition is affecting her ability to realize her full academic potential, but not to the extent that she is falling behind her peers? The SEN Code does not appear to address the needs of such children (DfES 2001a). Maybe, therefore, it would be wise to simply assume that a child with a medical condition is experiencing difficulty in learning until proven otherwise, in order to effect careful assessment of his learning needs.

The following case example illustrates how easily learning needs can go unrecognized in children where there are no obvious effects of a medical condition on physical or cognitive functioning using the current definition of SEN.

Case example: Amy, 7 years

Amy has Myalgic Encephalomyelitis (ME). She recently recommenced attendance at school following a long period of absence, resulting in the need for home tuition. To all intents and purposes, Amy looks as fit and healthy as the next child, but she is by no means fully recovered. She still

---

gets very tired on exertion and finds it extremely difficult to concentrate and remember things. She continues to function at a substantially lower level than she did prior to the onset of her illness. Amy is finding it difficult to complete her class work and keep up with her peers, so much so that she is feigning illness in the hope of being able to stay at home so she can have home tuition again. No one has picked up on Amy's difficulties.

Responding to the SEN of children with medical conditions

Children with medical conditions with suspected or actual SEN are subject to the underlying principles and procedures set out in the SEN Code of Practice for identifying, assessing and making provision for children's SEN, regardless of the underlying reason for these, and for supporting parents and children through SEN processes. The remainder of this chapter will therefore, out of necessity, convey information in a mainly generic, rather than specific fashion.

It is important to note that children have a very important voice in all matters relating to their SEN. Indeed, the United Nations Convention on the Rights of the Child states that children who are able to form opinions have a right to share those opinions and to have them taken into account in all matters concerning them. This right is upheld by the SEN Code of Practice through its assertion that, wherever feasible, children with SEN should be involved in decisions concerning their education, including which school they should attend and their learning targets, for example (DfES 2001a). The Code also states that children should contribute to any assessment of their needs. Children can convey their views through their parents or another family member if they wish, or through a professional who may be involved with them or another pupil.

There is absolutely no doubt that parents know the most about their child and have a vital role in supporting their child's education. It is therefore crucial that they too be listened to and have their views taken into account by anyone with responsibility for assessing and providing help to children with SEN. Indeed, government guidance and legislation relevant to SEN, notably the SEN Code of Practice and the 1996 Education Act, guide and support parents' involvement in the assessment and management of their child's SEN (DfES 2001a). Systems exist, such as 'disagreement resolution services' and the Special Educational Needs Tribunal (SENDIST), to support parents wishing to disagree with or formally appeal against LA decisions (these will be discussed later in this chapter). Furthermore, recent years have seen the development of independent organizations that support parents in communicating information about their child's needs and in expressing their views throughout SEN processes and procedures. Early years practitioners, as part of their work with parents of children with SEN, must ensure that parents are aware of the various support channels available to them. While the LA has a duty to inform parents of some of the support available, this does not cover all possible avenues. It is up to practitioners therefore to ensure that parents do not miss out on any potentially useful sources of support.

The SEN Code of Practice sets the following 'graduated response' to SEN:

Assessments for children over two but under compulsory school age:

This category encompasses part of the Foundation Stage which refers to education provision, wherever it occurs, for children aged three to five years.

Early Years Action
This is initiated when early years practitioners recognize a child as having SEN. Practitioners must put in place interventions that are additional to or different from those which are provided as part of the standard curriculum. Parents must be informed by the setting that their child is to receive such special educational provision due to having SEN. This should be done sensitively and in a way that makes it clear to parents that their contribution, in terms of sharing their knowledge and understanding of their child, is crucial to her progress. Parents should also be informed and consulted with regard to the need for any additional action. If practitioners and parents decide that a child does indeed require further support due to limited progress, then they must seek the advice of the Special Educational Needs Coordinator (SENCO) before deciding on the nature and content of any future intervention.

Early Years Action Plus
This refers to the involvement of external support services, or specialist advice being sought, to aid

a child's development through advice on interventions and target setting, more specialist assessments, advice on the use of specialist strategies or materials and the provision of support for certain activities. Support from external services is likely to be sought when the SENCO, in consultation with parents and colleagues, decides that, in spite of individualized intervention and support, the child:

♦ Continues to make little or no progress in specific areas over a long period

♦ Continues working at an early years curriculum substantially below that expected of children of a similar age

♦ Has emotional or behavioural difficulties which substantially and regularly interfere with the child's own learning or that of the group, despite having an individualized behaviour management programme

♦ Has sensory or physical needs, and requires additional equipment or regular visits for direct intervention or advice by practitioners from a specialist service

♦ Has ongoing communication or interaction difficulties that impeded the development of social relationships and cause substantial barriers to learning

(DfES 2001a: 37–8).

Requests for a statutory assessment
This takes place when Early Years Action Plus fails to meet a child's additional needs. The setting, along with

the parents and any external agencies involved, must consider whether a statutory assessment is required (the statutory assessment process will be discussed later on in this chapter). However, government-funded early education settings, other than maintained nursery schools or nursery classes within maintained schools, only have a statutory right to request an assessment for four and five year olds attending the setting.

Assessments for children attending full-time compulsory education in school

Some children with SEN may not have had their needs identified prior to commencing compulsory education. Formal assessment in schools follows a similar pattern to that which occurs in pre-school educational settings:

School Action
This refers to the provision of interventions for a child identified as having SEN that are, 'additional' to or 'different' from those provided as part of the standard curriculum. Parents should be informed and consulted on the implementation of School Action and also regarding any further action, should this be required. Prior to the implementation of interventions under School Action, it is likely that differential learning opportunities have been in place but that, despite these, a child:

◆ Makes little or no progress even when teaching approaches are targeted, particularly in a child's identified area of weakness

♦ Shows signs of difficulty in developing literacy or mathematics skills which result in poor attainment in some curriculum areas

♦ Presents persistent emotional or behavioural difficulties which are not ameliorated by the behaviour management techniques usually employed in the school

♦ Has sensory or physical problems, and continues to make little or no progress despite the provision of specialist equipment

♦ Has communication and/or interaction difficulties, and continues to make little or no progress despite the provision of a differentiated curriculum

(DfES 2001a: 52–3)

School Action Plus

This equates with Early Years Action Plus and refers to a request for help from external services or specialists. A decision to implement School Action Plus should be a joint one involving the parents and SENCO and other professionals involved with the child.

Children in receipt of special educational provision under School Action or School Action Plus must have an Individual Education Plan (IEP) which is used to record a child's targets, supportive interventions and teaching strategies to be used, and criteria against which progress can be measured. IEP's must be reviewed at least biannually.

Statutory Assessment of SEN

Where 'Early Years Action Plus' or 'School Action Plus' are not enough to meet a child's additional needs, then the setting, along with the parents and any external agencies involved, must consider whether to make a request to the LA for a statutory assessment of SEN. Parents can also request a statutory assessment, however, the LA must still consult with all the professionals working with a child.

Statutory assessment refers to a comprehensive multi-professional assessment of a child's needs and how to address them and may lead to a written statement of SEN; it is a legal document which outlines the details of a child's special needs and the special educational provision which the LA considers necessary to meet them.

A statutory assessment can include input from a range of education, health and social work professionals. Also, as part of the assessment, the LA must seek and consider the views of the parents, the child and the setting on the child's SEN. Parents are also requested to provide a report. This is called 'Parental Advice' and should include details of the professionals parents would like the LA to obtain information from, information relevant to their child's needs and any views on how these should be met. LAs are required to issue guidance to parents on how to record their advice and to give details of a named officer who can assist with this process. The named officer is the person responsible for an individual child's case and can be contacted for other more general advice relevant to a child's statutory assessment. As well as providing guidance for the recording of Parental

Medical Conditions

Advice and facilitating support from a named officer, LAs should give details of the local Parent Partnership Service who can also assist parents in recording Parental Advice. The wider role of Parent Partnership Services will be discussed later in this chapter under the heading 'support for parents'.

Following receipt of a request for a statutory assessment, the LA must request evidence of the child's difficulties and that of any intervention put in place for that child that has been maintained for a reasonable period of time, but to no avail. Where a child does not attend an early education setting, the LA must still endeavour to gather as much information as possible before determining whether an assessment is necessary. Once all the evidence is in place, the LA must then decide whether the child's difficulties can only be addressed through a statement of SEN.

LAs must respond to a request for a statutory assessment in accordance with the following timescale:

♦ The LA has six weeks to decide whether or not to undertake a statutory assessment and must inform the child's parents in writing that they are considering whether a statutory assessment is necessary. Parents must be given 29 days by the LA to present their views on why they think their child should be assessed. The 29 days counts towards the six weeks the LA has to decide whether or not to proceed with an assessment.

♦ The LA has ten weeks to carry out an assessment and decide whether or not to produce a statement in writing.

♦ If, following an assessment, the LA decides to issue a statement in writing, a proposed statement must reach the child's parents within two weeks of that decision, together with copies of all the reports on which it is based. The proposed statement should contain details of the child's SEN and how they will be met, details of any non-educational needs, for instance, the need for medication or some other form of medical treatment, and information pertaining to any non-educational provision by health or social services, for example, and how this will be met. It should also include information on the sort of school that would best meet the child's needs, however, the proposed statement does not specify a particular school. Instead, parents are encouraged to record on the proposed statement whether they would prefer their child to attend a mainstream or special school. Where parents express a preference for their child to attend a mainstream school, the LA is duty bound, under the Education Act 1996, to respect this wish unless the child's inclusion in mainstream would compromise the education of other children. In other words, LAs can only refuse to admit a child with a statement of SEN into a mainstream school if others' education would suffer as a result.

When scrutinizing the proposed statement, parents need to ensure that it:

♦ lists all their child's needs and difficulties

♦ lists all the provision needed by their child

♦ specifies the number of hours of extra help to be provided

Medical Conditions

- includes details of any special equipment the child will need

- is written in clearly understood language (parents should highlight any words or phrases they do not understand and ask for an explanation)

- specifies how all the needs which have been identified are to be met and by whom
  (Adapted from Contact a Family 2006: 5).

Where an LA decides not to issue a statement, it may issue a 'Note in Lieu of a Statement'. This contains acknowledgement of a child's SEN and describes the necessary provision to meet these needs, much like a statement does. A 'Note in Lieu of a Statement', however, is not legally binding and states that the child's SEN can adequately be met at Early Years or at School Action Plus, depending on the child's age. Like a proposed statement, a 'Note in Lieu of a Statement' must include copies of all the reports collated during the statutory assessment process. On issuing a 'Note in Lieu of a Statement', LAs must provide parents with details of how to appeal against their decision and of local disagreement resolution services, which are independent and informal services provided by LAs to resolve disagreements between parents and the LA or educational setting. LAs must also inform parents about disagreement resolution services in the event of a decision not to proceed with a statutory assessment and when issuing a proposed statement or revised proposed statement (below).

- Parents have 15 days to deliver their views to the LA on the proposed statement, or they can request a meeting with an LA officer to discuss its contents and proposals. A further meeting can be requested as long as this is done within 15 days of the first meeting. Indeed, several meetings can be requested providing that requests are always made within 15 days of the previous meeting. The LA, however, may decide that they cannot complete the final statement within the time limits. Once the last meeting has taken place, parents have 15 remaining days to submit any opposing views they may still have on the proposed statement to the LA. It is important to note, however, that whilst the LA may revise the statement to take account of parents' views, it is under no obligation to do so. A revised proposed statement will include a named school or alternative educational provision.

♦ The LA has 8 weeks to finalize the proposed statement. The final statement must include details of the child's special needs and outline the type of special educational provision needed to address them. It must also include details of a school or alternative educational provision for the child. LAs must ensure that the educational provision outlined in the statement is put in place from the date on which the statement is made.

Statements must be reviewed annually, other than those issued for children under two years of age. The annual review provides a forum for discussing a child's progress and whether or not changes to the statement are required in light of progress or otherwise or in view of changing needs. The annual review must give due consideration to the views of the child and of the parents.

Assessments for children under two

It is acknowledged that in a minority of cases, where there are severe and complex needs, requests for assessment may be made prior to the commencement of formal early education. Children under two years of age diagnosed with a major long-term illness or particular condition, for example, may be referred, having first obtained parental consent, to the LA for an assessment of SEN. Referrals are often made by health professionals working with the child or, in some cases, are instigated by practitioners working in early years settings such as Sure Start programmes. Parents can also request an assessment, in which case, under Section 331 of the Education Act 1996, it must be undertaken. The statutory assessment procedures pertinent to children over two need not apply in these cases. Instead, the assessment is undertaken in such a manner as the LA considers appropriate. Children in this age group are rarely issued a statement in writing, however, the LA must determine, in consultation with parents, the nature of special educational provision required. This may take the form of home-based programmes such as Portage, centre-based support or a combination of the two. LAs must ensure that regular monitoring takes place and must work in collaboration with child health services and social services where appropriate.

Where, on the rare occasion, a statement is issued on behalf of a child under two, it will outline the following:

- The child's needs

- The views of parents and professionals

- Details of the help to be provided

- Details of how help will be monitored and reviewed

It can be seen that drawing up a statement is a laborious process, which can sometimes result in a somewhat inflexible document that cannot respond to frequently changing needs in the same way as an IEP can. A written statement does enable, however, settings to access additional resources via the LA that may prove crucial to a child's educational success. Moreover, it allows parents additional placement request rights, including the right to request that their child attends a school in another authority and/or to ask for their child to attend a special school. LAs can refuse a placement request, however, where the requested school is already full, where the choice of placement is not considered the best option for the child, and/or, as mentioned earlier, where a child's attendance in a particular setting may prove detrimental to others' education. According to the Education and Skills Select Committee (2006), 3 per cent of children with SEN have a written statement, contrary to the 20 per cent quoted by Baroness Warnock in her recent criticisms of the statementing process and other aspects of SEN policy (Warnock 2005) – see Chapter 1. The number of statements issued varies between LAs from 1 to 5 per cent. Thus it would appear that children with the same needs are subject to different levels of provision, which is clearly unacceptable. It has been argued that this is largely due to the absence of clear criteria for deciding whether to issue a statement (House of Commons Education and Skills Select Committee 2006). The government has called for a reduction in the reliance on statements by some authorities. Unfortunately however, this has led, in some instances, to the development of a blanket policy of no longer issuing statements, which is unlawful and has resulted in the DfES having to remind LAs of their responsibilities (Bovell 2006).

Parental dissatisfaction with the statutory assessment process and statements is common-place. Some parents have reported SEN processes and procedures causing so much stress and anxiety as to take over their lives (House of Commons Education and Skills Select Committee 2006). This is highly unsatisfactory given that many parents of children with SEN, especially where there are associated medical conditions and/or disability, already face ongoing disruption to day-to-day living, as well as having to deal emotionally with their child's difficulties. The last thing parents need is a system for supporting SEN that causes added stress. Reported areas of discontent include:

♦ LAs being unwilling to issues statements

♦ Inaccurate statutory assessments by biased profes-sionals who are not independent from the LA

♦ Vague allocation of resources by LAs, which parents feel is done deliberately so that LAs can 'wriggle out' of their responsibilities

◆ Bad placement decisions

◆ Transfer of statement problems where children move to a different authority. The statement cannot move with them due to LAs having different methods of assessment and resource allocation

(House of Commons Education and Skills Select Committee 2006: 44)

Support systems

Fortunately, there exists nowadays, a wide range of supportive mechanisms for parents of children exposed to SEN processes. Parents can access information relevant to their acting on any concerns they may have about their child's developmental progress. They can gain practical support in articulating information about their child's difficulties when requesting a statutory assessment, and are entitled to practical and emotional support during the assessment process itself.

Where parents are unable, for whatever reason, to communicate their child's needs effectively, then these may go unrecognized and therefore unmet; a parent's request for a statutory assessment may be inappropriately declined or, if accepted, be poorly informed. Support, in some cases, is therefore absolutely imperative. Parents may also need support in their right to appeal against LA decisions where they are in disagreement with these. Indeed, LAs have a duty to inform parents of their right to appeal and how to go about this. They also have a duty to provide parents with information on accessing support during the statutory assessment process.

Early years practitioners are ideally placed to signpost parents in the direction of organizations that provide general support for parents of children with SEN, which may include children with medical conditions, as well as offering support themselves. Early years practitioners can also ensure that parents of children with medical conditions, who are not considered to have SEN, know what to do if they suspect that their child is experiencing difficulties with regard to learning.

Discussion/reflection

♦ What systems are in place in your setting to ensure that parents know what to do if they suspect their child has SEN? Are these adequate? If not, how can they be improved?

♦ Are all practitioners working in the setting sufficiently aware of support systems available to parents of children with SEN? If not, how can this be addressed in order to raise awareness?

♦ Are parents overtly encouraged to express to practitioners the concerns they may have about their child's progress/well-being?

♦ Do practitioners make a point of referring parents of children with SEN to the SEN Code of Practice and make sure that they know how to obtain their free copy?

♦ Does the setting provide DfES guidance leaflets for parents of children with SEN? If so, are they located so that they are easily accessible to parents?

♦ How well do practitioners work in partnership with children with SEN and their parents? (see Chapter 6).

What should parents do if they suspect their child has SEN?

Where parents are concerned about the development of their pre-school age child, who has not commenced formal early years education, their first port of call is the child's general practitioner or health visitor. Either of these professionals can advise on what steps should be taken to access assessment and appropriate intervention.

In the case of children attending early years education settings, concerned parents are advised to express their concerns to the pre-school/nursery or classroom teacher and head teacher as appropriate. They can also obtain advice from a special educational needs co-ordinator (SENCO) a member of the teaching staff with designated responsibility for coordinating help for children with SEN. Parents can talk over their concerns with the teacher and SENCO, both of whom can advise on and mobilize the most appropriate response based on guidance contained in the SEN Code of Practice (DfES 2001a).

A parent who suspects their child may have SEN can also obtain support from their local 'parent partnership service' which can be contacted via the LA or the National Parent Partnership Network (see useful contacts below). Parent partnership services provide advice about SEN and information on the options available to parents. They also provide guidance relevant to SEN procedures and processes. An extremely useful and valued resource provided by parent partnership services is the support of an independent parental supporter, a trained volunteer who, under the guidance and supervision of the parent partnership service, helps parents through SEN procedures. Independent parental supporters can, among other things, help aid parents' understanding of issues relevant to their child's SEN and associated procedures; however, making decisions about a child is not part of their remit which is to:

◆ Listen to parents' worries and concerns

◆ Provide parents with ongoing general support

◆ Help parents understand what is happening during SEN procedures and processes such as School Action, assessment and statementing

◆ Explain to parents their rights and responsibilities

◆ Help parents prepare for and attend visits and meetings

◆ Help with phone calls, filling in forms and writing letters and reports

◆ Help parents express their views and communicate with schools and LAs

◆ Help parents find further sources of information, support and advice

(www.directgov.uk)

Other sources of support for parents of children with SEN

The Advisory Centre for Education (ACE) also provides advice and information to parents about SEN, as does the Independent Panel for Special Educational Needs (IPSEA). The latter provide comprehensive advice to parents on issues relating to the statutory assessment process and a child's statement, including for example: requesting a statutory assessment or reassessment; requesting a change to the named school on a child's statement; complaints procedures and asking for an early review. IPSEA also provide extremely useful model letters designed to help parents communicate various issues relevant to their child's SEN to the LA.

Another useful source of advice and guidance for parents of children with suspected or actual SEN is Contact a Family (CAF), a charitable organization set up to support families of disabled children. CAF provide information on specific conditions and on rare disorders and have recently produced a very useful factsheet outlining parents' rights and the procedures for identifying, assessing and intervening in children's SEN. This can be obtained from the CAF website below.

Appealing LA decisions

As already mentioned, LAs must inform parents of their right to appeal decisions relevant to the statutory assessment process and statement, and how to go about this. Appeals are heard by an independent body, namely the Special educational Needs Tribunal (SENDIST). Parents who have made an appeal to SENDIST are advised to maintain negotiation with the LA.

Useful contacts

Action for ME
Telephone: 0845 123 2314
Website: www.a4me.org.uk

Advisory Centre for Education (ACE)
Telephone: 020 7704 3370
Website: www.ace-ed.org.uk

Contact a Family
Telephone: 0808 808 3555
Website: www.cafamily.org.uk

Independent Panel for Special Education Advice (IPSEA)
Telephone: 0800 018 4016
Website: www.ipsea.org.uk

DfES (for a free Copy of the SEN Code of Practice and to obtain information leaflets for parents)
Telephone: 0845 602 2260
Website: www.teachernet.gov.uk/sen

National Parent Partnership Network
Telephone: 020 7843 6058
Website: www.parentpartnership.org.uk

Special Educational Needs and Disability Tribunal (SENDIST)
Telephone: 0870 241 2555
Website: www.sendist.gov.uk

4

Legislation and Policy

There exists little by way of legislation and policy that is relevant specifically to children with medical conditions. Their needs are addressed to some extent, however, in generic legislation and policy concerning children. Moreover, as readers will be aware at this point, many children with medical conditions have associated SEN and/or disability and are, as such, affected by legislation and policy relating to these areas. This chapter will outline some key generic, specific and SEN and disability legislation and policy affecting children with medical conditions. It does not, however, purport to present a definitive account of this area. Neither will it revisit legislation that was covered in the first chapter.

Learning outcomes

When you have read this chapter you should be able to:

♦ Identify key legislation and policy affecting children with medical conditions

♦ Understand some of the implications for practice of the said legislation and policy

♦ Locate pertinent documents for use in settings

♦ Access further information as required

The Children Act 1989

Children with medical conditions, disabled children and those with SEN, regardless of whether or not these overlap, come within the scope of the Children Act 1989 since, without services, they would be unable to enjoy a 'reasonable standard of health or development'. As such, they should benefit from children's service plans, in terms of services which are additional to those provided to children on a universal basis.

The Act defines a child as being in need if:

a) he is unlikely to achieve or maintain or have the opportunity of achieving or maintaining a reasonable standard of health or development without the provision for him of services by an LA

b) his health or development is likely to be significantly impaired, or further impaired, without the provision for him of such services; or

c) he is disabled [the Act recognizes chronic illness as a subset of disability]

(Children Act 1989, S17 (10))

The Children Act 1989 places a duty on LAs to provide services for children who are disabled, and their families, aimed at minimizing the effect of the disability. It also requires that a register be kept by social services of children with disabilities as a basis for planning services and also as a means of providing information to families.

SEN and the Education Act

As already mentioned in Chapter 3, section 312 of the Education Act 1996 defines SEN. Section 322 places a duty on local health services to provide assistance to the LA for a child with SEN, including advice and training for staff in dealing with a child's medical needs. Health services are exempt from such duties under certain circumstances; these are outlined in the Act.

Disability legislation

Current legislation relevant to disability in childhood, much of which covers adults as well, pertains either specifically to disability or to issues relevant to both disability and SEN, almost as if they necessarily overlap, which of course they do not. Note that many of the children covered by the following disability legislation will have a medical condition:

♦ The DDA 1995 incorporates several legal rights affecting disabled individuals, including the right to reasonable access to goods, facilities, premises and services. Under Part 3 of the Act, early years settings, including childminders and other private, voluntary and statutory provision, that are not constituted as schools, are required to make 'reasonable adjustments' to facilitate the inclusion of children with disabilities. Schools are also required to make such adjustments. The making of 'reasonable adjustments' constitutes one of the two key duties of the DDA; the second concerns less favourable treatment of children with disabilities. Settings are required not to treat a disabled child 'less favourably' than any other child for reasons associated with his disability. Failure to heed one or other of these two duties can amount to unlawful discrimination.

♦ The Disability Rights Commission is an independent body established by an Act of Parliament to put a stop to discrimination against disabled individuals and to provide for equal opportunities.

♦ The Special Educational Needs and Disability Act 2001 extends disability discrimination to education.

♦ The Carers and Disabled Children Act 2000 grants parents and carers the right to an assessment of their own needs. It also makes available financial assistance, in the form of vouchers and direct payment, for carers of disabled children, but only when they have been assessed as needing a service.

Health and safety legislation

♦ The Health and Safety at Work Act 1974 (HWSA) places duties on employers to safeguard the health and safety of their employees and others on the premises. In early years settings this covers staff, children and visitors, including parents. The employer is usually the LA. Most early years settings will, at one time or another, have children on roll with a medical condition. Under the HWSA, the responsibility of the employer is to ensure that safety measures take account of the needs of *all* children attending the setting, which may involve making special arrangements for some children. Under the National Standards for day-care settings (DfES 2003a), the registered person must comply with all relevant health and safety legislation and take action to promote safety.

◆ The Management of the Health and Safety at Work Regulations 1999, made under the HWSA, require employers to: make an assessment of the risks of activities, introduce measures to control these risks and to tell their employees about these measures. It is important to note that both the HWSA, and the Management of Health and Safety at Work Regulations also apply to employees, who must: take reasonable care of their own and others health and safety, cooperate with their employers, carry out activities in accordance with training and instructions and inform the employer of any serious risk.

◆ The Control of Substances Hazardous to Health Regulations 2002 requires employers to control exposures to hazardous substances; this includes medicines that are harmful to anyone to whom they are not prescribed.

◆ The Manual Handling Operations Regulations 1992 requires employers to assess the risks associated with manual handling and to put systems in place to minimize these.

♦ The Provision and Use of Work Equipment Regulations 1998 covers an employer's duty to ensure that equipment is safe, suitable and only used following instruction and training.

Children with medical conditions can be more at risk than other children attending a setting, in which case practitioners may need to employ additional health and safety measures. Where individual procedures are required, it becomes the employer's responsibility to ensure that practitioners are knowledgeable in and suitably trained to deliver them.

Other relevant legislation

♦ The Misuse of Drugs Act 1971 has relevance for settings where a child has been prescribed a controlled drug.

♦ The Medicines Act 1968 specifies the way that medicines are prescribed, supplied and administered in the UK.

♦ The Education (School Premises) Regulations 1999 require schools to have a suitable room for use for medical purposes.

Policy

Every Child Matters

Heralding the government's vision for children's services, *Every Child Matters*, and *Every Child Matters: Next Steps*, hereafter called *ECM* and *ECM: Next Steps* respectively, recognize the government's commitment to enabling all children to:

1 Be healthy

2 Stay safe

3 Enjoy and achieve

4 Make a positive contribution; and

5 Enjoy economic well-being
(DfES 2003c, DfES 2004b)

Very importantly, *ECM* and *ECM: Next Steps* acknowledge the long-term benefits of early intervention for children who need support, either on an intermittent or an ongoing basis, and stress the need for health, education and social care services to improve information sharing and assessment with the aim of facilitating the earliest possible intervention for children with additional needs of whatever kind; this includes needs arising from medical conditions.

The *Every Child Matters: Change for Children* programme, from hereon in called *ECM: Change for Children*, sets out action that needs to be taken locally to realize not only the five outcomes, but also, the government's ambition for integrated service delivery and early intervention (DfES 2004c).

81

Medical Conditions

The National Service Framework for Children, Young People and Maternity Services (NSF)

The *NSF* represents a key policy area relevant to children with medical conditions and their families (DH and DfES 2004). It sets out a ten-year programme to stimulate long-term and sustained improvement in children's health and well-being. It forms an integral part of the *ECM: Change for Children* programme that will contribute to the attainment of improved outcomes for all children, young people and maternity services. The *NSF* is concerned with meeting the needs of children who are well, as well as those who are acutely or chronically ill and/or disabled.

NSF Standards

Standard 6 is concerned with the requirements of children and young people who have, or are at risk of developing, a long-term medical condition. This does not include conditions which are disabling. The needs of disabled children are addressed in standard 8, together with the needs of children and young people with complex health needs. It is recommended that standards 6 and 8 be read in tandem in light of the fact that the needs of children and their families are not always clearly defined (DH and DfES 2004a). It can be seen that standards 7, 9 and 10 are also relevant to children with medical conditions. It is advised that these more specialist standards be read in conjunction with standards 1 to 5 (the core standards) which cover areas that apply to all children, young people and their families. Standard 11 is concerned with the health and well-being of mother and

Core Standards (1–5)	Particular Needs (6–10)	Maternity Services (11)
1. Promoting Health and Well-being, Identifying Needs and Intervening Early 2. Supporting Parenting 3. Child, Young Person and Family-centred Services 4. Growing Up into Adulthood 5. Safeguarding and Promoting the Welfare of Children and Young People	6. Children and Young People who are Ill 7. Children in Hospital 8. Disabled Children and Young People and those with Complex Health Needs 9. The Mental Health and Psychological Well-being of Children and Young People 10. Medicines for Children and Young People	11. Maternity Services

baby before or during pregnancy, throughout birth and during the first three months of parenthood.

Standards 6 to 10

Standard 6: 'Children and Young People, who are Ill'

All children and young people who are ill, or thought to be ill, or injured will have timely access to appropriate advice and to effective services which address their health, social, educational and emotional needs throughout the period of their illness. (DH and DfES 2004a: 4)

This standard sets out the government's vision for children who are ill or injured. It wants to see:

Medical Conditions

♦ Children and young people who are ill receiving timely, high-quality and effective care as close to home as possible

♦ Children and young people who are ill and their families being cared for within a local system which coordinates health, social care and education in a way that meets their individual needs
(DH and DfES 2004a: 4)

It also highlights, as a marker of good practice, that health care be delivered in such a way as to promote participation in education, thereby maximizing a child or young person's potential. Indeed, a section of the NSF is concerned solely with issues relevant to supporting children's educational needs, where it is stated that:

♦ Children and young people who have either an acute or a prolonged illness are at risk of missing out on educational opportunities due to prolonged absences from school

♦ Health and education services must work together in a supportive, coordinated way to support the child or young person to develop and achieve their full educational potential. This includes developing processes for effective communication about the needs of individual children and supporting the re-integration of a child back into school

♦ Systems need to be developed to ensure that health and social services provide information, training and support to schools and early years settings, in caring for children with medical needs

♦ There is evidence to demonstrate that children living in disadvantaged areas or communities are more likely to have increased absences from school due to poor health. This is a particular concern as it will contribute to a cycle of poor education, low-paid employment and ill-health

(DH and DfES 2004a: 25)

The section goes on to explore various ameliorative steps. These will not be outlined here however; rather, they will be discussed in Chapter 5.

Standard 7: 'Standard for Hospital Services' (DH 2003)

Standard 7 was published in advance of the rest of the children's NSF in order to meet the government's pledged response to the recommendations of the Kennedy report (2001) on the inquiry into children's heart surgery at the Bristol Royal Infirmary during 1984–95. Consequently, the format of this standard differs to that of the other 10 standards of the NSF. The overarching standard is presented as an aim:

To deliver hospital services that meet the needs of children, young people and their parents and provide effective and safe care through appropriately trained and skilled staff working in suitable child friendly environments. (DH 2003: 8)

Standard 7 acknowledges that being admitted to hospital is daunting for most children and also gives rise to concern for parents and relatives. It therefore sets out the government's vision for improving the way hospitals care for children so that they 'can get on with the important business of childhood' (DH 2003: 1). It covers:

♦ The design and delivery of hospital services around the needs of children and their families

♦ The safety of children while they are in hospital

♦ The quality of services for children in hospital

♦ The suitability of hospital settings for the care children receive

(DH 2003: 1)

Emphasis is placed upon meeting children's basic need for play and recreation whilst visiting or staying in hospital. It is also acknowledged that play should be used for therapeutic purposes as part of a child's care plan to aid the assimilation of new information, enable children to cope with being in a potentially frightening environment, prepare children for medical procedures and interventions and to accelerate recovery (DH 2003: 14).

Meeting the ongoing educational needs of children staying in hospital is seen as a priority. It is recommended that, where a child's schooling is affected by his condition, hospital staff maintain close liaison with and involve the school as early as possible lest his educational achievement be compromised (DH 2003). The standard also recognizes the entitlement of all three and four year olds to early education and, to this end, stipulates that hospitals included on the LA's Directory of Providers should receive funding for this (DH 2003).

Standard 8: 'Disabled Children and Young People and those with Complex Health Needs'

> Children and young people who are disabled or who have complex health needs receive co-ordinated high quality child and family-centred services which are based on assessed needs, which promote social inclusion. And where possible, which enable them and their families to live ordinary lives. (DH and DfES 2004b: 8)

This standard addresses the needs of children with learning difficulties, autistic spectrum disorders, sensory impairments, physical impairments and emotional/behavioural disorders. It is cross-referenced with standard 6 and sets out the government's vision for children who are disabled or have complex health needs thus:

We want to see:

♦ Children and young people who are disabled, or have complex health needs, supported to participate in family and community activities and facilities

♦ Health, education and social care services organized around the needs of children and young people and their families, with coordinated multi-agency assessments leading to prompt, convenient, responsive and high quality multi-agency interventions that maximize the child's ability to reach his or her full potential

♦ Children and young people and their families actively involved in all decisions affecting them and in shaping local services

(DH and DfESb 2004: 5)

87

Medical Conditions

Standard 9: 'The Mental Health and Psychological Well-Being of Children and Young People'

All children and young people, from birth to their eighteenth birthday, who have mental health problems and disorders have access to timely, integrated, high quality, multi-disciplinary mental health services to ensure effective assessment, treatment and support, for them and their families. (DH and DfESc 2004: 4)

Standard 9 addresses the mental health needs of children and young people. It sets out the government's vision for these individuals and their families thus:
We want to see:

♦ An improvement in the mental health of all children and young people

♦ That multi-agency services working in partnership promote the mental health of all children and young people, provide early intervention and also meet the needs of children and young people with established or complex problems

♦ That all children, young people and their families have access to mental health care based upon the best available evidence and provided by staff with an appropriate range of skills and competencies
(DH and DfES 2004c: 4)

Standard 9 states that *all* staff working with children and young people, in whatever capacity, should be enabled to recognize the contribution they can make to children's emotional well-being and social development and to support children in the event of concern for their well-being. It states also that staff must appreciate their duties with regard to supporting children in difficulty (DH and DfES 2004c).

Standard 10: 'Medicines for Children and Young People'

Standard 10, as its name suggests, is concerned with issues relevant to the use of medicines for children and young people:

> Children, young people, their parents or carers and health care professionals in all settings make decisions about medicines based on sound information about risk and benefit. They have access to safe and effective medicines that are prescribed on the basis of the best available evidence. (DH and DfESd 2004: 4)

In line with this standard, the government wants to see:

♦ All children and young people receiving medicines that are safe and effective, in formulations that can easily be administered and are appropriate to their age, having minimal impact on their education and lifestyle

♦ Medicines being prescribed, dispensed and administered by professionals who are well trained, informed and competent to work with children to improve health outcomes and minimize harm and any side effects of medicines

♦ Children and young people and their parents or carers who are well informed and supported to make choices about their medicines and are competent in the administration of medicines

(DH and DfESd 2004: 4)

Anyone administering medicine to a child or children attending an early years setting must observe the guidance set out in standard 10 (DH and DFES 2004d), together with that contained within *Managing Medicines in Schools and Early Years Settings* (DfES 2005), hereafter referred to as *Managing Medicines*.

Activity

Learn more about the NSF standards by visiting the DH website, www.dh.gov.uk/policyandguidance/ healthandsocialcaretopics/childrenservices

---

Managing Medicines (DfES 2005)

Managing Medicines, which replaces previous guidance from the Department for Education and Employment and the Department of Health, *Supporting Pupils with Medical Needs: A good practice guide* (DfEE/DH 1996) and *Circular 14/96 Supporting Pupils with Medical Needs in School* (DfEE/DH 1996), provides guidance for LAs, NHS Primary Care Trusts, schools, early years settings and families on:

◆ The development of policies and procedures for supporting children with medical conditions, with the aim of ensuring that everyone, as well as parents, has a clear understanding of their respective roles

◆ The establishment of effective management systems aimed at supporting children with medical and other health needs

◆ How to ensure that medicines are handled responsibly within early years settings, including schools

◆ How to manage a medical emergency affecting a child within a school or other early years setting

Managing Medicines (DfES 2005) was produced by the Department for Education and Skills in conjunction with the Department of Health and takes full account of the recommendations in the Children's *NSF*. It currently represents another key policy area relevant to children with medical conditions. Indeed, every early years setting should have their own copy and be familiar with its contents. Free copies are available via the teachernet website at www.teachernet.gov.uk/publications or from DfES publications on telephone number: 0845 60 222 60

Access to Education for Children and Young People with Medical Needs (DfES and DH 2001b)

Access to Education sets out minimum national standards for the education of children who are unable to attend school either due to the nature or severity of a medical condition or because they require some form of treatment, possibly in hospital, which precludes their attendance at school for a significant period of time. The aim is to ensure that children and young people with needs arising from medical conditions experience the absolute minimum of disruption to schooling through the continuation of education as far as is possible within the constraints of their condition. The emphasis is on continuing learning in light of its importance to children's future mental and physical development. The guidance addresses the needs of children with physical and/or mental health issues, including children with life threatening or terminal illnesses.

Access to Education stipulates that LAs, as part of their responsibilities towards children who are unable to attend school because of illness, should ensure that:

♦ Pupils are not at home without access to education for more than 15 working days

♦ Pupils who have an illness/diagnosis which indicates prolonged or recurring periods of absence from school, whether at home or in hospital, have access to education, so far as possible, from day one

♦ Pupils receive an education of similar quality to that available in school, including a broad and balanced curriculum

♦ Pupils educated at home receive a minimum entitlement of five hours teaching per week. This is a minimum and should be increased where that is necessary to enable a pupil to keep up with their studies

(DfES 2001b: 8)

Whether or not a child makes use of this education should depend not only on medical advice, but also on his ability to cope with learning activities during periods of illness. Although children must be encouraged to study, under no circumstances must they be put under any pressure to do so if there is any indication that they are not well enough.

LAs are required to ensure that a pupil is not absent without access to teaching for more than 15 working days, including any period that a child has spent in hospital (DfES 2001b). Where a child has been in hospital for a longer period and has received teaching as an inpatient, then LAs should recognize the disruption to the continuity of education for that pupil and the need to make education available as soon as possible following discharge (DfES 2001b).

Access to Education provides guidance on: the type and range of provision for children unable to access education via the usual route; developing policies, procedures and standards of provision; ensuring early identification and intervention; maintaining continuity of educational provision; supporting reintegration; partnership working; delivering high quality education and issues relevant to accountability.

The guidance builds on examples of best practice and aims to realize the following key principles reproduced here in light of their significance:

♦ All pupils should have access to as much education as their medical condition allows so that they are able to maintain the momentum of their education and to keep up with their studies (p. 5).

♦ All parties should be aware of their roles and responsibilities and be clear about the standards of service that are expected of them. Policies should be clear, transparent and accessible to all (p. 10).

♦ A child or young person who is unable to access education due to medical needs should have their educational needs identified and receive educational support quickly and effectively (p. 13).

♦ The aim of any provision should be to provide continuity of education similar to that provided at the pupil's home school (p. 17).

♦ The education of pupils with medical needs is a partnership. It is essential that education, health and other agencies work closely together to provide the support to enable a pupil with medical needs to receive appropriate education (p. 22).

♦ Each long-term pupil should have an assessment of their situation and the provision of well-structured support from the home school in liaison with the hospital and the home-teaching service and other agencies as necessary to assist reintegration to school, wherever possible (p. 27).

♦ Parents should be full collaborative partners and should be informed about their child's educational programme and performance. Children also have a right to be involved in making decisions and exercising choice (p. 31).

♦ A pupil who has medical needs should have equal opportunities with their peer group, including a broad and balanced curriculum. All such pupils should as far as possible receive the same range of quality of educational opportunities as they would have done at their home school (p. 34).

◆ Arrangements should be in place to ensure adequate monitoring and evaluation

(DfES 2001b)

Access to Education represents another key policy area relevant to children with medical needs. The document should therefore be available in all formal education settings to support children during periods of absence and to guide the successful reintegration of children into school and can be obtained via the DfES website at www.dfes.gov.uk/sickchildren or by telephoning DfES publications on 0845 60 222 60.

The SEN Code of Practice (DfES 2001b)

As stated periodically throughout this book, many children with medical conditions will have SEN. Thus the SEN Code of Practice will be of relevance to them, their families and anyone with responsibility for the assessment and management of SEN.

Policy relevant specifically to children with disabilities

Support in the early years is crucial to the development and future life chances of disabled children. It has long been assumed, however, that policies designed to support the general child population also encompass the needs of disabled children and their families whereas in reality they do not.

Recent policy though, *Improving the Life Chances of Disabled People* (DWP, DH, DfES 2005), reflects long-awaited acknowledgement by the government of the fact that, historically, its policies have failed to meet the needs of disabled children and their families and that support should be more targeted. It is envisaged that, by 2025, young disabled children and their families will be able to 'access "ordinary" lives, through effective support in mainstream settings' (DWP, DH, DfES 2005: 101), three and four year old disabled children will be able to access and benefit form early education by 2010 and that, by 2015, under five year old children and their families will finally receive and benefit from high-quality and affordable childcare provision. Such provision has long been lacking resulting in parents of disabled children having no option but to stay at home despite, in many cases, a financial need and/or a desire to work.

Improving the Life Chances of Disabled People also identifies a need for:

♦ Services that are 'fit for purpose' in terms of workforce, joint working and information about disabled children's needs

♦ Disabled children and their families to have timely access to the equipment they need, when and where they need it

♦ A key worker for all families with high needs to provide information, improve communication and coordinate multi-agency interventions

(DWP, DH, DfES 2005: 101)

Other key policy areas relevant to addressing the needs of disabled children and their families and which early years practitioners should not only familiarize themselves with, but also use to inform and direct practice, include:

♦ *Together from the Start: Practical guidance for professionals working with disabled children (birth to third birthday) and their families* (DfES 2003b). As its title suggests, this policy document contains a set of guidance for professionals working with very young disabled children on how best to meet children's and families' needs. It also provides guidance on service delivery and early diagnosis.

♦ *The Early Support Pilot Programme* (ESPP). A government-funded national initiative announced in May 2002 and currently (at the time of writing) undergoing evaluation. Its aims are to provide support to disabled children under two and their families through service integration, improved information sharing and assessment and key worker support, by following the guidance in 'Together from the Start' (DfES 2003b).

♦ Standard 8 of the aforementioned Children's *NSF* is concerned with disabled children and young people (and those with complex health needs). Also, the Department of Health (DH) has published very useful guidance to be used in tandem with Standard 8 in the form of a Complex Disability Exemplar (DH 2005) which maps out the experience of a fictional child (Maria), diagnosed with cerebral palsy, and her family through to her adulthood.

Useful resources

www.changeforchildren.gov.uk
www.dfes.gov.uk
www.dh.gov.uk
www.hmso.gov.uk/acts.htm

5

Supporting Children with Medical Conditions and their Families

This chapter will outline some of the roles and responsibilities of early years practitioners, their employers, health personnel and other professionals in supporting children with medical conditions in early years settings. The chapter does not offer practical guidance on the management of specific conditions. Neither does it provide a step-by-step guide to the undertaking of specific medical/clinical procedures. Both of these areas are covered very well elsewhere (DfES 2005, Carlin 2005). Instead, the chapter will provide a general overview of the provision of supportive environments which adopt a holistic and individual approach and which build on children's strengths and resilience rather than focus on a condition. Reference will be made to partnership working, the need for clear policies and procedures and training implications.

Learning outcomes

After reading this chapter, you should be able to:

♦ Outline the advantages of high-quality support for children with medical conditions and their parents

Medical Conditions

♦ Understand why partnership working is essential for effective support

♦ Give examples of policies and procedures needed in settings to effect adequate support of children with medical conditions and their families

♦ Describe training implications

Supporting children

Children with medical conditions want, and have the potential, to prosper both socially and academically as much as their peers. Many can only realize such aspirations and potential, however, in the presence of high-quality and sustained support within education and care settings. The overall aim of such support should be to guarantee children's optimum health within settings, to maximize their access to the National Curriculum and other opportunities as appropriate (and often taken for granted by most), and to secure their successful inclusion within mainstream education and care settings. Inadequate support can have the opposite effect; it can compromise children's attainments and well-being and lead to segregation within mainstream settings (see Chapter 1).

Early years practitioners have a very important role not only in relation to supporting children with medical conditions and their parents within mainstream provision, but also in fostering positive attitudes towards these children. When seen to fully include all children and to handle crises calmly and reassuringly, practitioners will benefit not only the child concerned but also others within the setting, staff and children alike. It must be noted, however, that even with the best will in the world, practitioners cannot adequately support and include children with medical conditions unless they themselves are supported in this role by their employer, usually the LA, in terms of the allocation of appropriate and sufficient resources and guidance. In other words, providers of education and care cannot rely on the good will of practitioners alone to implement and sustain, for children with medical conditions, high-quality inclusive education and care.

When supporting children with medical conditions, it is important to remember that they are often more vulnerable in settings than their 'healthier' counterparts. This, I hasten to add, is as much, if not more, a result of inadequate support systems as it is the effects of a medical condition. Children with medical conditions might experience ongoing or intermittent discomfort due to pain, nausea or some form of irritation. They may face constant fear or anxiety associated with deterioration, or uncertainty as to whether or not their needs will be met and by whom. Sadly, children with medical conditions are more likely than most children to fall victim to peer rejection and bullying. This may be because, due to absence, they never quite become part of a peer group, or, for some children, it might arise from the fact that they look different as a result of their condition. Whatever the reasons, as covered in Chapter 2, such stress/vulnerability is set to compromise children's physical, social and emotional well-being and thereby their educational progress. Support must therefore, as well as catering for children's physical needs, aim to counter these stressors. This can only be achieved, however, where practitioners exercise constant vigilance over children's day-to-day experiences in a setting so that any problems can be spotted early on and ameliorative steps put in place.

Settings vary in their response to children with medical needs and their families. Some offer laudable levels of practical and emotional support to children and parents alike; others, unfortunately, and for a variety of reasons, are rejecting, both on the part of practitioners and other children attending the setting. Medical needs may or may not be met. Some formal education settings enable children to keep up with the work of their classmates during periods of absence whereas others do not, causing, in some instances, children to fall irreversibly behind with their school work. In a paper presented to the British Educational Research Association Annual Conference on an investigation into the support needs of children with long-term health conditions attending mainstream schools, Lightfoot and Wright (1999: 4) commented that 'support appeared idiosyncratic rather than systematic, a matter of luck according to the ethos of the individual schools and attitudes of individual teachers and NHS staff'. They also highlighted that where support was lacking, pupils experienced difficulties such as not being believed that they had symptoms; being excluded form certain activities without cause or, conversely, being inappropriately made to engage others (Lightfoot and Wright 1999).

As well as needing support in their endeavour to play and learn alongside their peers, children with medical conditions also value feeling supported. Data gathered from school children demonstrates that support in the following areas is particularly valued:

♦ Minimizing the impact of absence (e.g. sending work home)

♦ Minimizing exclusion from aspects of school life (e.g. access to classrooms; adapting social activities; going on school trips)

♦ Easing difficulties with peers (e.g. intervention when bullied)

♦ Emotional support (someone to talk to when worried)

♦ Having teachers who understand – who know about the condition, understand its impact on school life and make any special arrangements needed (most valued)

(Lightfoot and Wright 1999: 3)

With reference to the third bullet point, Closs (2000: 102–4) provides very useful guidance for practitioners on supporting children's peer relationships. Parents also appreciate feeling supported by practitioners engaged in educating and caring for children within settings. They particularly value being listened to; having their worries about their child's health and/or progress acknowledged; practitioners fully utilizing information that they (the parents) provide; having a named contact in the setting, someone influential and reliable, and being promptly informed of any delay in their child's educational progress (Norris and Closs 1999).

Medical Conditions

The disruption to normal day-to-day life brought about by a medical diagnosis affecting a child can often, however, make parents difficult to deal with. Practitioners must therefore remain mindful of what parents may be going through, such as anxiety and depression, lack of sleep, financial constraints, child-care problems, time constraints and so on. This will enable practitioners to empathize with parents' plight and thus be more accepting of the odd negative remark. Practitioners should be overt in their appreciation of parents' difficulties and should attempt to put them in touch with organizations that might be able to offer some support. It is important to note also that, where effective provision is in place, parents can feel secure in the knowledge that their child will benefit from attending a setting both socially and educationally, and that their experience of the setting will be a positive one; thus avoiding more stressors, including concern over a child's educational progress, the standard of care he is receiving and his happiness. Poor service provision on the other hand, especially on the part of education, has been reported as a major stress factor to parents of children with medical needs; more so than problems associated with child care (Beresford 1994)

Activity

Draw up a list of difficulties that can be encountered by parents of children with medical conditions. Seek out national and local support groups/organizations that may be able to help and keep an easily

---

accessible directory of these in your setting. Make sure this is updated on a regular basis.

Supporting children with medical conditions and their families can prove both challenging and very rewarding. Challenging because sustained support requires a great deal of practical and emotional effort, together with meticulous planning and continuing empathy. Rewarding because of the sense of achievement and satisfaction that comes from contributing to a child's happiness and success.

The provision of high-quality support for children with medical conditions and their families is dependent upon:

♦ Effective multi-agency and multi-disciplinary partnerships

♦ Collaborative work with children, where they are mature enough, and parents

♦ The existence in settings of clear policies and procedures, based on LA interpretation of national policies and guidance

♦ Confident, knowledgeable and suitably trained practitioners

♦ Sufficient and appropriate resources.

Multi-agency partnerships

Multi-agency partnership working refers to joint working on the part of education, health and social services, and possibly the voluntary sector, on the formulation of policies and procedures relevant to supporting the education and care of children, in this instance, with medical conditions. Representatives from each of the services should meet regularly to develop, review and update such policies and procedures. These must reflect current legislation and national policy (see Chapter 3) and should also take account of the recommendations, based on day to day experience of working with children and their families, of frontline staff, including, for example, teachers and other early years practitioners, nurses and doctors. Policies and procedures should also reflect recent medical developments, as well as local needs and provision. Once developed or updated, policies and procedures should be disseminated to local schools and early years settings, to governing bodies and to management groups.

Carlin (2005) explains why a multi-agency approach to the development of policies and protocols is necessary. A joint approach:

♦ Promotes consistency of approach across a local authority area and gives status to that approach

♦ Ensures the commitment of all agencies to providing shared governance and shared ownership of the process

♦ Draws on the expertise and knowledge of staff in all agencies

♦ Ensures that the roles and responsibilities of agencies are clearly defined

♦ Reduces the confusion for parents about what tasks schools and early years settings can and cannot take on

♦ Helps to clarify the entitlement to a level of support a child with medical conditions [sic] may expect

(Carlin 2005: 11)

Multi-disciplinary partnership working

Multi-disciplinary partnership working, in this instance, refers to effective joint working on the part of frontline practitioners involved in the education and care of children with medical conditions and is aimed at affording children the best possible outcomes in terms of their diagnosis, educational progress and their emotional and behavioural well-being. A myriad of practitioners can be involved in the care and education of a child with a medical condition, especially where there are associated SEN and/or disability, including, for example, teachers, nursery nurses, SENCOs, educational psychologists, health visitors, school nurses, school doctors, community paediatricians, speech therapists, community nurses, specialist nurses, specialist doctors, learning support workers, social workers and so on. Wherever possible, practitioners must work together on the assessment of a child's needs, the planning of strategies to meet those needs and on evaluating the effectiveness of such strategies. Multi-disciplinary working allows for role clarification and information sharing, thereby contributing to coordinated care.

Working in partnership with parents and children

Working in partnership with parents and children makes for policies and procedures that are truly tailored towards meeting individual children's needs, in line with a child and family-centred approach. Children with medical conditions, and their families, are often extremely knowledgeable about their child's condition and so can contribute a great deal to ensuring that medical needs arising from these are adequately met. Practitioners should respect this expertise and be prepared to learn from it. Indeed, settings should encourage parents and children to share their know-how.

Settings can facilitate successful partnership work with parents and children by:

♦ Meeting with the child (where she is mature enough) and her parents prior to commencement at a setting, or immediately following diagnosis where attendance has already commenced, to discuss the child's needs and how these can be met and by whom. Both the parents and the child should be encouraged to express any fears and anxieties they may have and to share any relevant information pertaining to the child's condition. The meeting should be attended by senior practitioners working in the setting, relevant health personnel, the SENCO and learning-support worker(s), as appropriate.

♦ Ensuring that children and parents are made to feel welcome at the setting and that they are secure in the knowledge that every effort will be made to meet the child's needs

♦ Making explicit the fact that practitioners and other members of staff are approachable

♦ Informing children, if at an appropriate age, and their parents of the settings' policies and procedures for supporting children with medical conditions

♦ Ensuring that information for parents is written in plain language and information for children in child-friendly language

♦ Developing individual policies and procedures in consultation with children and parents that accommodate their views

♦ Ensuring that parents are allocated a key contact person

♦ Arranging meetings with parents where they are given plenty of advance warning and where any logistical problems or difficulties are accommodated for

♦ Encouraging parents to attend and participate in meetings and training concerning their child

♦ Sharing news about a child's progress and achievements, and not just about problems

♦ Encouraging children to take responsibility for their own medical needs, as far as is practicable, and any decisions relating to them

Clear policies and procedures

Carlin (2005), in *Including Me: Managing complex health needs in schools and early years settings*, provides comprehensive and welcome guidance on the formulation of local policies and procedures relevant to the needs of children with medical conditions attending schools and early years settings. Indeed, every setting should have its own copy. Copies are available for purchase from the Council for Disabled Children (www.ncb.org.uk/cdc or Tel: 020 7843 6334). *Managing Medicines* (DfES 2005) and *Access to Education* (DfES 2001b) are also highly pertinent to the development of policies and procedures for supporting children with medical needs and can be obtained via the DfES website (www.dfes.gov.uk or Tel: 0845 60 222 60).

All early years settings catering for the needs of children with medical conditions should have a medical needs policy. This can take the form of a stand-alone document or, alternatively, it can form part of an overall inclusion, health and safety or medicines policy. A medical needs policy will:

♦ Demonstrate the commitment to positively promoting the inclusion of children with medical conditions [sic]

♦ Lead to a clear understanding of the roles and responsibilities of staff within a school or early years setting

♦ Clarify for parents and children what they can expect from the school or early years setting and what is expected from them

(adapted from Carlin 2005: 14)

Supporting Children with Medical Conditions

A medical needs policy should contain information on:

◆ The roles and responsibilities of staff with regard to supporting children with medical conditions

◆ What the school or early years setting expects from the parents in terms of being kept informed and updated about their child's medical needs

◆ The training which staff can expect to receive prior to supporting a child with a medical condition

◆ Indemnity or insurance arrangements

◆ Risk management, record keeping and protocols to be followed

◆ Responses to emergency situations

◆ Any additional arrangements which need to be put in place for activities which take place away from the usual school or at another setting site

(adapted from Carlin 2005: 14–15)

Individual Health Care Plans (IHCPs)

IHCPs are intended to assist the identification by staff of the necessary safety measures that should be taken to support children with medical conditions, and to avoid unnecessary risk both to the child and others in the setting. IHCPs contain specific arrangements for supporting individual children and must conform to standard policies and procedures. An IHCP should include the following:

◆ Details of the child's condition

Medical Conditions

♦ Particular procedures that should be carried out, including who should carry them out and the training they should expect

♦ Information on the manner in which the child prefers any task to be carried out, in order to ensure consistency of approach across all settings attended by the child

♦ Parental wishes for the child

♦ Any needs which may affect the child's use of services, such as transport or play activities, implementation of therapy programmes, etc

♦ Any anticipated changes in the child's condition or care routine

♦ Any side-effects of medicines taken by a child

♦ What constitutes an emergency

♦ What action to take in an emergency

♦ What not to do in the event of an emergency

♦ Who to contact in an emergency

♦ The use, storage and maintenance of any equipment

♦ Any arrangements for the provision of education or associated services when the child is too unwell to attend school or is in hospital or another health-care setting

♦ Protocols for exchanging information between agencies (with clearly defined lines of responsibility and named contacts)

(Adapted from: DfES 2005 and Carlin 2005: 39)

Supporting Children with Medical Conditions

Developing an individual health-care plan should be the combined effort of the child's parent or carer, relevant health professionals and possibly:

◆ The head teacher or head of setting

◆ The child (if appropriate)

◆ Early years practitioners/class teachers

◆ Care assistants or support staff (if applicable)

◆ Staff who are trained to administer medicines

◆ Staff who are trained in emergency procedures
(DfES 2005)

Medical needs policies and IHCPs are required to address the needs of all children with medical conditions attending an early years setting and do not apply to 'well' children; not directly anyway. Settings should also have in place specific policies and procedures for the admission and transition to another setting of children with medical conditions, and also for supporting absence brought about by long-term illness.

It goes without saying that early years settings must plan carefully for the admission of a child with a medical condition, or for his transition to another setting. Smooth admission bodes well for successful inclusion. Settings should plan ahead, allowing themselves, as far as is practicable, ample time for any additional adaptations to be made, staff to receive appropriate training and for the employment and training of additional support staff (Carlin 2005). In the event of transition, the receiving setting should be informed of a child's impending admission well in advance of when this will happen so that they too have time to make all the necessary arrangements.

The Hackney Learning Trust and the City and Hackney Teaching Primary Care Trust (cited in Carlin 2005: 22–3) has developed an extremely useful pre-admission/transition checklist for schools, which could easily be adapted for use by other early years settings. It considers the following:

◆ How will the child get to school?

◆ How will the child get around the building, into classrooms, toilets?

◆ What issues arise for school outings?

◆ Will quiet, distraction-free workspaces and/or dinner times be necessary and available?

◆ At what level are the child's self-help skills, such as eating, drinking, toileting?

◆ What equipment will be needed?

◆ Does the child have medical needs?

◆ What issues arise for the child at play times and lunch, for example, friends, equipment, not coping with noise in the dining hall?

◆ How will the child access curriculum levels? Notify curriculum coordinators in relation to planning and providing resources?

◆ Does the child need adult support – in the classroom, at lunch, at play time, around the school?

♦ What additional skills will adults need in relation to learning, social and emotional, physical and medical needs? What is the plan for training the staff?

♦ How many additional people will need to be trained if the child needs assistance with feeding or toileting?

♦ What preparation is necessary for all staff, children and parents before the child starts?

Frequent and/or prolonged periods of absence from settings of a child with a medical condition can give rise to anxiety affecting both the child and his parents. There are often concerns regarding the possible faltering of educational progress and the feasibility of catching up with missed school work. Where pupils have faltered significantly in terms of keeping up, it may be necessary to narrow the curriculum to afford catch up in the core subjects. There is often anxiety also, surrounding whether or not the child will still 'fit in' with his friends following prolonged or frequent separation from them, and around the child's capacity to cope with returning to school following prolonged absence. A one-off absence, for some reason, even where this is prolonged, seems to have less effect on a child's progress. Moreover, practitioners tend to be more accommodating of a one-off period than they are of frequent recurrent absences.

> ### Case example: A teacher talking about a pupil with recurrent kidney infections
>
> 'It's a shame for him and us, we just start him on something and he seems to get hold of it, then off he goes again for another two days or three weeks, so it's one step forward and two steps back, again and again. It's all very tiresome and after a bit you lose heart and, shamefully really, stop trying. If only he would just go off, really get better, then come back and stay back.'
>
> (Closs and Norris 1999: 3)

Mainstream schools have a number of responsibilities in relation to pupils who are absent due to illness. They should:

♦ Have a policy and a named person responsible for dealing with pupils who are unable to attend school due to a medical condition

♦ Notify the LA and Education Welfare Officer if a pupil is, or is likely to be, away from school due to a medical condition for more than 15 working days

♦ Supply the appropriate education provider with information about a pupil's capabilities, educational progress and programmes of work

♦ Be active in the monitoring of progress and in the re-integration into school, liaising with other agencies, as necessary

♦ Ensure that pupils who are unable to attend school because of a medical condition are kept informed about the school's social events, are able to participate, for example, in homework clubs, study support and other activities

♦ Encourage and facilitate liaison with peers, for example, through visits and videos

(DfES 2001b: 8)

Children with medical conditions differ in terms of their needs; for example, some need special diets, some require treatment that is invasive, others need specific support on trips and outings, while others need transport to and from school. Policies and procedures on these and other more specific needs must also be in place in early years settings, as appropriate. As mentioned earlier, Carlin (2005) provides very useful guidance on the development of such policies and procedures.

Generic policies and procedures

While children with medical conditions are supported by policies and procedures that affect them specifically, they are also naturally covered by generic policies and procedures that apply to all children and sometimes others, including staff and visitors, in a setting, such as a setting's health and safety policy or medicines policy, for example. Because the need for the administration of medicine is relatively common in children with medical conditions, it is deemed necessary, at this juncture, to discuss some issues relevant to the development of a medicines policy.

Early years employees are not legally obliged to administer medicines to children or to supervise the self-administration of medication by a child (DfES 2005). However, anyone caring for children, including early years practitioners, have a common-law duty of care to ensure the health and safety of all children in their charge. This could extend to administering medicine (DfES 2005). Employees working within registered day care are subject to conditions of employment that are unique to each particular setting. As such, it is the responsibility of the registered person to arrange who should administer medicines. This may well, although not necessarily, be written into the relevant employee's contract of employment. In practice, the administration of medicine and supervision of self-administration are frequently undertaken activities, aimed at facilitating attendance, and must be done in accordance with the relevant government guidance namely *Managing Medicines* (DfES, 2005).

Managing Medicines states that a medicines policy should cover:

♦ Procedures for managing prescription medicines which need to be taken during the school day

♦ Procedures for managing prescription medicines on trips and outings

♦ A clear statement on the roles and responsibilities of staff managing administration of medicines, and for administering or supervising the administration of medicines

- A clear statement on parental responsibilities in respect of their child's medical needs

- The need for prior written agreement from parents for any medicines to be given to a child (for early years settings prior permission is a mandatory requirement)

- The circumstances in which children may take non-prescription medicines

- The school or setting's policy on assisting children with long-term or complex medical needs

- Policy on children carrying and taking their medicines themselves

- Staff training in dealing with medical needs

- Record keeping

- Safe storage of medicines

- Access to the school's emergency procedures

- Risk assessment and management procedures
  (DfES 2005: 7)

Standard 7 of the government's National Standards for Under 8's Day Care and Childminding (DfES 2003a), which sets minimum standards of day care, provides guidance for staff working in day care settings on the development of policy relevant to the administration of medicines to children in their care. It states that:

- Medicines are stored in their original containers, clearly labelled and inaccessible to children

Medical Conditions

♦ Medicines are not usually administered unless they have been prescribed for that child by a doctor

♦ The parent gives prior written permission to administer the medication (this is a mandatory requirement)

♦ Written records are kept of all medicines administered to children, and that parents sign the record book to acknowledge an entry (this is a mandatory requirement)

♦ If the administration of prescription medicines requires technical/medical knowledge then individual training is provided for staff from a qualified health professional. Training is specific to the individual child concerned.

(DfES 2003a: 19)

The National Standards document recommends that this guidance be followed in conjunction with similar but more comprehensive guidance issued by OfSTED (2001).

The need for confident, knowledgeable and suitably trained practitioners

Often, practitioners are daunted at the prospect of including children with a medical condition in their setting, especially where their needs are complex. This is most likely the outcome of non-existent or inadequate staff development whereby practitioners lack the necessary levels of knowledge and skills that are prerequisite to supporting these children in any meaningful way. Inadequately prepared practitioners may also fear being held accountable for any mishaps, such as incorrect administration of medication or failure to recognize and deal with a medical emergency. It is important to point out, therefore, that practitioners supporting children with medical conditions, where this is done in accordance with employers' policies and procedures, would not be liable for any adverse events. Indeed, employers must make sure that their insurance arrangements provide full cover for staff acting within the scope of their employment.

Practitioners can become knowledgeable about medical conditions affecting children in their setting via self-directed research, by obtaining information from parents, through effective liaison with health professionals and by means of suitable, high-quality training. Chapter 2 contains information relevant to self-directed research, including where to seek information from and what sort of information to look up.

Parents or persons with parental responsibility have the ultimate responsibility for their child's health and should therefore provide schools and other early years settings with information relevant to their child's medical condition. Some parents have difficulties, however, in understanding their child's condition. In such cases, practitioners can refer parents to their general practitioner or heath visitor for further clarification, in the case of pre-school age children, or to a member of the school health service, where a child is attending compulsory education.

Health professionals – for example the child's health visitor, who is the main health contact for pre-school settings – and members of the school health service, including the school nurse and the school doctor, should also provide early years practitioners with information about medical conditions affecting children in their setting. Where a community paediatrician and/or a specialist nurse is/are involved in the care of a child, they too can provide early years practitioners with relevant background information. It must be remembered, however, that health professionals must not disclose information pertaining to a child's illness without first obtaining parents' consent.

Information about a child's medical condition from health professionals can, however, be difficult to come by. For example, there is evidence to suggest that communication and collaboration between health and education professionals, relevant to addressing the needs of children with long-term medical conditions but degree of statement of SEN, is low (Mukherjee *et al.* 2001, Larcombe 1995). The information sharing of hospital-based doctors has been found to vary widely, with some providing prompt information thus enabling support systems to be put in place, while others communicate information eventually or not at all (Dyson *et al.* 1998).

The following have been found to present barriers to effective liaison:

♦ Confusion among teachers about which health professionals to approach for advice and information

♦ Lack of direct contact with a pupil's lead professional

♦ Lack of multi-agency meetings for pupils without a statement of SEN

♦ Refusal by some health professionals to share information with teachers on the grounds of confidentiality

♦ Some health professionals do not perceive teachers as their partners in caring for children

(Mukherjee *et al.* 2001)

Primary and secondary school teachers who took part in one of the aforementioned studies reported receiving limited information from NHS staff as being a major obstacle to their understanding (Mukherjee *et al.* 2000). They reported feeling ill-informed about issues relevant to a range of medical conditions, including the more common asthma, diabetes and epilepsy. It is reasonable to surmise that such a lack of awareness extends beyond the compulsory school setting to other early years settings, although currently there is no evidence to support this assertion.

Self-assessment exercise

If you work or are a student in an early years setting, try to elicit the following:

♦ When a child in the setting has a medical condition, who is the person who provides information to practitioners about the child's progress, the effects of the condition on the child's daily living and any specific needs the child may have?

♦ How is this information communicated, for example, by phone, letter or with face-to-face contact?

Medical Conditions

♦ What means of communication do practitioners prefer?

♦ Are practitioners kept up to date about changes in a child's condition?

♦ How soon after a child is diagnosed with a medical condition do practitioners receive information from a health professional?

♦ Is this information automatically forthcoming or must it be requested?

♦ Do practitioners feel sufficiently informed?

♦ Are practitioners made aware of whom to approach for advice?

♦ Do health professionals provide practitioners with training relevant to medical conditions affecting a child or children in the setting?

Obtaining answers to these questions will enable you to ascertain whether practitioners are suitably well informed by health professionals to support children with medical conditions or whether action is required to improve liaison.

The following model, developed by the Social Policy Research Unit of the University of York, can be used to address barriers to effective liaison between health personnel and early years practitioners (SPRU 2000). The model holds that settings should have:

♦ A named practitioner with responsibility for pupils with a medical condition

- A named health professional

- An individual health-care plan developed in accordance with relevant government guidelines for children with a medical condition

- Multi-agency meetings for children with complex needs arising from a medical condition

- A standard health register

- A *Smart Card* for school children with medical conditions

(adapted from: SPRU 2000)

The model requires that the named practitioner has designated responsibility for this group of children, including communicating with NHS and LA staff as appropriate.

The named health professional, the health visitor or the school nurse or school doctor, depending on the nature of the setting, will have responsibility for setting up a health register of children with medical conditions or health support needs, to be reviewed on a regular basis, for example, annually. The named health professional will also be responsible for coordinating the development, updating and reviewing of an individual health-care plan for each child with a medical condition.

Compulsory school age children may wish to carry a *Smart Card* containing any health information related to their condition that they might need to pass quickly and inconspicuously to teachers.

Suitably trained early years practitioners are crucial to the delivery of high-quality and efficient support to children with medical conditions attending early years settings. Practitioners should be trained not only in information about a condition and addressing physical needs, but also in listening, counselling and interpersonal skills. All personnel working with a particular child should receive training on a general level. Those supporting children on a one to one basis, however, must receive more specific training.

Non-medical personnel can be trained to undertake certain clinical procedures, including, for example, catheterization, stoma care and intramuscular or subcutaneous injection using a pre-loaded syringe. Delegation of such procedures must be done within a robust governance framework, however, to include: initial training and preparation of staff; assessment and confirmation of competence of staff; and confirmation of arrangements for ongoing support, updating of training and re-assessment of competence of staff (Carlin 2005: 47). Information relevant to which procedures can and cannot be delegated to non-medical staff is available from the Royal College of Nursing. Training on the undertaking of clinical procedures is generally delivered by nursing staff: mainly school nurses, specialist nurses and community children's nurses. The latter two tend to provide training on particularly complex care procedures. Health personnel delivering training to a non-medical early years practitioner must sign a statement of that person's competence in the undertaking of the relevant activity.

Early years practitioners involved in supporting children with medical conditions must also receive training in moving and handling and risk-assessment procedures, both on a general level and in relation to individual children's needs. Such training must be delivered by accredited trainers, and practitioners must be deemed competent by them prior to undertaking any moving and handling or risk-assessment activities.

Another useful resource

Annex B in *Managing Medicines* provides the following very useful forms that settings can use, either as they are or which can be modified in accordance with individual settings' policies on the administration of medicines:

- ◆ 'Contacting Emergency Services'
- ◆ 'Health Care Plan'
- ◆ 'Parental agreement for school/setting to administer medicine'
- ◆ 'Head teacher/Head of setting agreement to administer medicine'
- ◆ 'Record of medicine administered to an individual child'
- ◆ 'Record of medicines administered to all children'
- ◆ 'Request for a child to carry his/her own medicine'
- ◆ 'Staff training record – administration of medicines'
- ◆ 'Authorisation for the administration of rectal diazepam'

(DfES 2005)

Medical Conditions

All the forms are downloadable as word documents to facilitate personalization, at www.teachernet.gov. uk/medical

Conclusion

Children with medical conditions, in the presence of supportive responses, can enjoy optimal health, and can play and learn with their peers and gain maximum access to curricular and extra-curricular activities.

There exists, however, little by way of legislation and policy that is relevant specifically to children with medical conditions attending early years settings. Their needs are addressed in the main through generic legislation and policy concerning children and, where there is associated SEN and/or disability, by legislation and policy relating to these areas. As such, some children with medical conditions and their families remain vulnerable to discriminatory practice. For example, children with medical conditions have the same right of admission to early years settings as other children, as long as their condition does not compromise the health and safety of others. Unfortunately, however, this right is not always upheld. Some settings continue to refuse admission to children on the grounds of being unable to cater for their needs and, unless a child is deemed disabled under the terms of the DDA, are able to do so. Thus, it is reasonable to assert that for some children with medical conditions and their families, there exists a substantial shortfall in current anti-discriminatory legislation.

A medical condition does not in itself mean that a

Medical Conditions

child has SEN. Rather, it is the impact of the condition on the child's learning ability, social and emotional development that may bring about SEN. It is important to remember also, that the effects of a medical condition are not always palpable. As such, SEN may go undetected in some children.

A child with a medical condition with associated SEN, and his family, are covered by the processes and procedures set out in the SEN Code of Practice and the principles therein. Early years practitioners are ideally placed to support children and parents by implementing these. They can also direct families to support networks whose specific remit is to offer practical and emotional support during sometimes stressful and long, drawn-out SEN assessment, intervention and review processes.

Children with medical conditions have the same potential to prosper, both socially and academically, as their peers. Realizing such potential, however, is largely dependent on the provision by early years practitioners, their employers, health personnel and other professionals, working collaboratively with children and families, and of high quality, ongoing and sustained support in settings.

The challenge of supporting children with medical conditions cannot, however, be met by front-line staff and their employers alone. The time has come to conclude the long-standing mainstream versus special schools debate in favour of action, based on consultation with children with medical conditions, and their families, to ensure uniform high-quality inclusive education and care, whatever form this may take, for all children attending schools and early years settings.

References

Barker, P. (1993) 'The Effects of Physical Illness'. In V. Varma (ed.) *How and Why Children Fail*. Jessica Kingsley Publishers.

Beresford, B. (1994) *Positively Parents: Caring for a Severely Disabled Child*. London: HMSO.

Bolton, A. (1997) *Losing the Thread: Pupils' and Parents' Voices about Education for Sick Children*. National Associaltion for the Education of Sick Children.

Bovell, V. (2006) 'Time to spell out the line on special needs'. *Guardian Unlimited,* last accessed: 21 September 2006 at http://education.guardian.co.uk

Brain, D.J. and Maclay, I. (1968) 'Controlled study of mothers and children in hospital'. *British Medical Journal*, 1, 278–80.

British Paediatric Association (1995) *Health Needs of School Age Children*. London: BPA.

Carlin, J. (2005) Including Me: *Managing complex health needs in schools and early years settings*. Council for Disabled Children.

Closs, A. and Burnett, A. (1995) 'Education for children with a poor prognosis; reflections on parental wishes and on an appropriate curriculum'. *Child: Care, Health and Development,* 21, 387–94.

Closs and Norris (1997) 'Outlook Uncertain: Enabling the Education of Children with Medical Conditions'. *Spotlight from the Scottish Council for Research in*

Education, last accessed: 21 September 2006 at http://www.scre.ac.uk

Closs, A. (ed.) (2000) *The Education of Children with Medial Conditions.* London: David Fulton Publishers.

Contact a Family (2006) *Factsheet: Special Educational Needs.* England: CAF.

DfE (1994) *Code of Practice on the Identification and Assessment of Special Needs.* London: HMSO.

DfEE (1996a) *Supporting Pupils with Medical Needs in School. Circular 14/96.* London: HMSO.

DfEE (1996b) *Supporting Pupils with Medical Needs in School: a good practice guide.* London: HMSO.

DfES (2001a) *Special Educational Needs Code of Practice.* Nottingham: DfES Publications.

DfES (2001b) *Access to Education for Children and Young People with Medical Needs.* Nottingham: DfES Publications.

DfES (2003a) *National Standards for Under 8's Day Care and Childminding.* Nottingham: DfES Publications.

DfES (2003b) *Together from the Start: Practical guidance for professionals working with disabled children (birth to third birthday) and their families.* Nottingham: DfES Publications.

DfES (2003c) *Every Child Matters.* London: The Stationery Office.

DfES (2004a) *Removing Barriers to Achievement.* Nottingham: DfES Publications.

DfES (2004b) *Every Child Matters: Next Steps.* Nottingham: DfES Publications.

DfES (2004c) *Every Child Matters: Change for Children.* Nottingham: DfES Publications.

DfES (2005) *Managing Medicines in Schools and Early Years Settings.* Nottingham: DfES Publications.

DH (2003) *Getting the Right Start: National Service Framework for Children: Standard for Hospital Services.* DH Publications.

DH and DfES (2004a) *National Service Framework for Children, Young People and Maternity Services: Children and Young People who Are Ill.* DH Publications.

DH and DfES (2004b) *National Service Framework for Children, Young People and Maternity Services: Disabled Children and Young People and those with Complex Health Needs.* DH Publications.

DH and DfES (2004c) *National Service Framework for Children, Young People and Maternity Service: The Mental Health and Psychological Well-being of Children and Young People.* DH Publications.

DH and DfES (2004d) *National Service Framework for Children, Young People and Maternity Service: Medicines for Children and Young People.* DH Publications.

DH (2005) *Complex Disability Exemplar.* DH Publications.

Dyson, A., Lin, M. and Millward, A. (1998) *Effective Communication Between Schools, LEA's and Health and Social Services in the Field of Educational Needs.* Ipswich: DfEE Publications.

DWP, DH and DfES (2005) *Improving the Life Chances of Disabled People.* London: The Stationery Office.

Eiser, C. (1990) *Chronic Childhood Disease.* Cambridge, UK: Cambridge University Press.

Eiser, C. (2000) 'The Psychological impact of chronic illness on children's development' In: A. Closs (ed.)

The Education of Children with Medical Conditions. London: David Fulton Publishers.

Freud, A. (1966) *The Ego Mechanisms of Defense.* International Universities Press.

Goslin, E.R. (1979) 'The effect of crisis intervention therapy in reducing anxiety in emergency hospitalization of preschool children' Dissertation Abstracts International, 40.

House of Commons Education and Skills Select Committee (2006) *Special Educational Needs: Third Report.* London: The Stationery Office.

Kennedy, I. (2001) *Bristol Royal Infirmary Inquiry.* London: HMSO.

Larcombe, I. (1995) *Reintegration into School after Hospital Treatment.* Aldershot: Avebury.

Lightfoot, J., Wright, S. and Sloper, P. (1998) 'Supporting pupils in mainstream school with an illness or disability: young people's views'. *Child: Care, Health and Development,* 25 (4) 267–83.

Lightfoot, J. and Wright, S. (1999) 'Supporting pupils with special health needs in mainstream schools'. Paper presented at the British Educational Research Association Annual Conference.

McDermott, S., Coker, A.L., Mani, S., Krishnaswami, S., Nagle, R.J., Barnett-Queen, L.L. and Wuori, D.F. (1996) 'A population-based analysis of behaviour problems in children with cerebral palsy'. *Journal of Paediatric Psychology,* 21, 447–63.

Mukherjee, S., Lightfoot, J. and Sloper, P. (2000) 'The inclusion of pupils with a chronic health condition in mainstream school: what does it mean for teachers?' *Educational Research,* 42 (1) 59–72.

Mukherjee, S., Lightfoot, J. and Sloper, P. (2001)

'Communicating about pupils in mainstream school with special health needs: the NHS perspective'. *Child: Care, Health and Development*, 28 (1) 21–7.

National Association of Head Teachers (2003) SEN Policy Paper, last accessed 21 September 2006 at http://www.publications.parliamnet.uk

Norris, C. and Closs, A. (1999) 'Child and parent relationships with teachers in schools responsible for the education of children with serious medical conditions'. *British Journal of Special Education* 26 (1) 29–33.

O'Brien, J. and Forest, M. (1989) *Action for Inclusion: How to improve schools by welcoming children with special needs into regular classrooms.* Toronto, Ontario: Inclusion Press.

Ofsted (2001) *Crèches: Guidance to the National Standards.* London: The Stationery Office.

Ofsted (2004) The Annual Report of Her Majesty's Chief Inspector of Schools, last accessed 01 October 2006 at http://www.ofsted.gov.uk?publications/annualreport

Perrin, E.C. and Gerrity, B.S. (1981) 'There's a demon in your belly: Children's understanding of illness'. *Paediatrics*, 31, 841–49.

Prugh, D.G., Staub, E.M., Sands, H.H., Kirschbaum, R.M. and Lenihan, E.A. (1953) 'A study of the emotional reactions of children and families to hospitalization and illness' *American Journal of Orthopsychiatry*, 23, 70–106.

Rossen, B.E. and McKeever, P.D. (1996) 'The behaviour of preschoolers during and after brief surgical hospitalizations'. *Issues in Comprehensive Pediatric Nursing*, 19, 121–33.

Sebba, J. and Sachdev, D. (1997) *What Works in*

Inclusive Education. Barnardos (www.barnardos. org.uk/resources).

SPRU (2000) Improving Health/Schools Communication for Pupils with Special Health Needs. University of York.

UNESCO (1994) The Salamanca Statement on Inclusive Education, last accessed 21 September 2006 at http:// www.unesco.org/education/pdf/SALAMA_E.PDF

Varni, J.W., Katz, E.R., Colegrove, J.R. and Dolgin, M. (1994) 'Perceived social support and adjustment of children with newly diagnosed cancer'. Journal of Developmental and Behavioural Paediatrics, 15. 20–6.

Vessey, A. and Mebane, D.J. (2000) 'Chronic Conditions and Child Development'. In P. Ludder Jackson and J.A. Vessey (eds) Child with a Chronic Condition. Mosby.

Wallander, J.L. and Varni, J.W. (1998) 'Effects of Pediatric Chronic Physical Disorders on Child and Family Adjustment'. Journal of Child Psychology and Psychiatry, 39 (1) 29–46.

Warnock, M. (1978) Report of the Committee of Enquiry into the Education of 'Handicapped' Children and Young People. London: HMSO.

Warnock, M. (2005) Special Educational Needs: A New Look, Impact No. 11. London: Philosophy of Education.

Wolff, S. (1981) Children Under Stress (2nd Edition). London: Penguin Books.